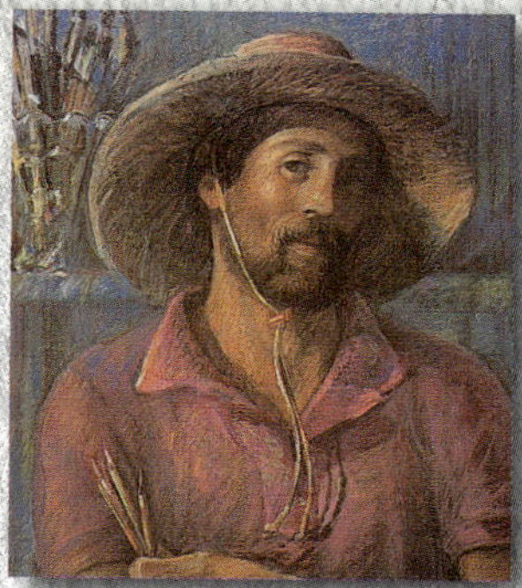

Portraits

The vibrancy and versatility of pastels make them ideal for capturing the subtle nuances of a subject's personality in a realistic portrait. And because pastels are available in literally thousands of shades, you can accurately paint any skin tone or eye color that exists. In this book, you'll discover how to select colors to make a variety of flesh-tone palettes, and you'll learn how to apply basic pastel strokes and techniques. Artist Ken Goldman also offers helpful advice about setting up poses, working from life and from photographs, and designing a pleasing composition. In addition, he introduces you to the fundamentals of color theory, color harmony, simplified anatomy, and basic proportions. You'll even explore ways to use pastels with other media, such as watercolor and charcoal. By following along with the colorful demonstrations in this book, you'll soon develop all the skills you need to begin creating your own realistic portraits in pastel.

Walter Foster

BASIC MATERIALS

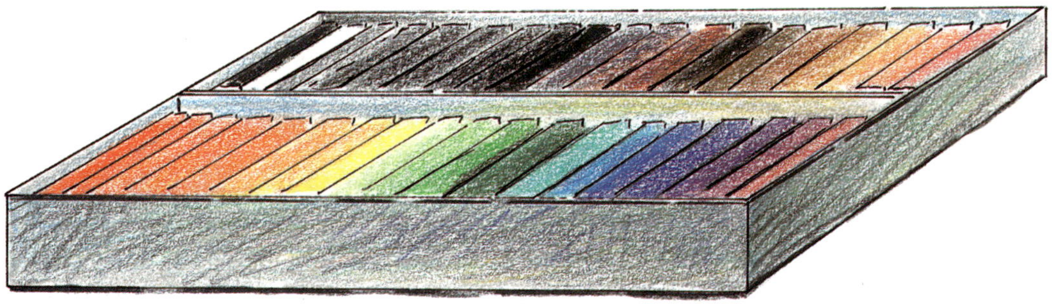

Hard Pastels—Hard pastels (single or double box) are useful at any stage. Sharpen them to a point for details, or break the sticks and use them on edge to apply broad areas of color. Since they are less expensive than soft pastels and do not wear down as quickly, they are especially helpful at the beginning of a portrait for an overall lay-in of color.

Soft Pastels—A good stick of soft pastel goes onto paper like soft butter onto bread. Light colors easily cover dark colors, and bright colors can transform dull colors at any stage. You can get by with a small set, but the lack of value range can be limiting. The wider your choice of values and colors, the greater your possibility for unrestricted expressiveness. I recommend a set of at least 100.

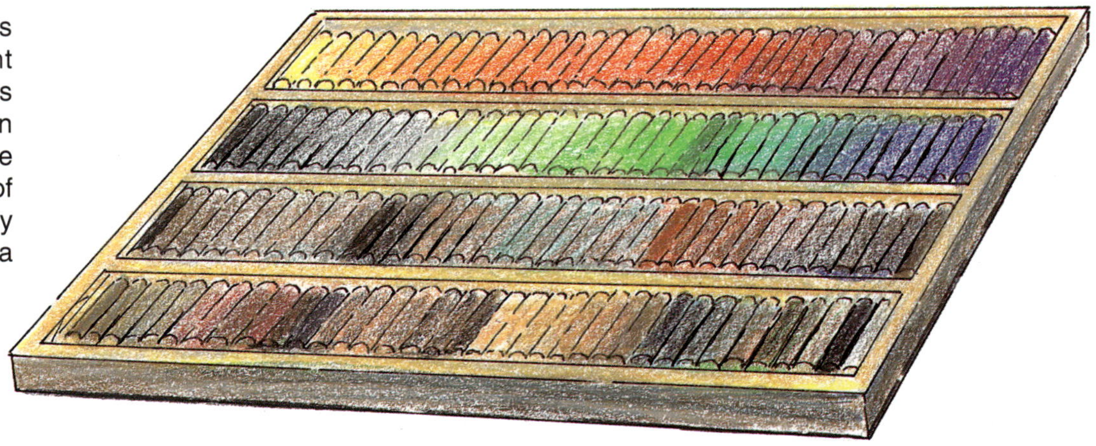

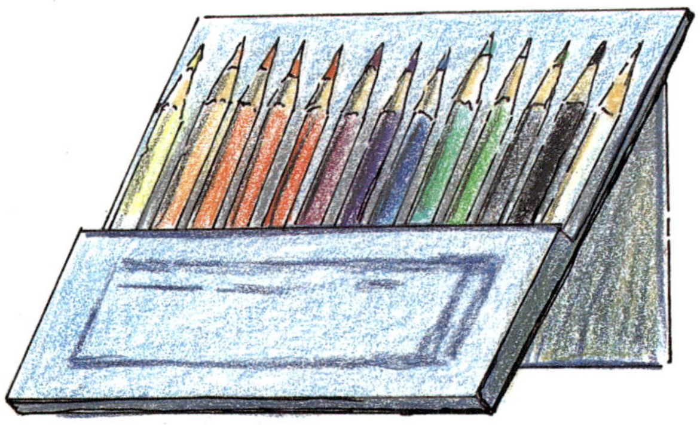

Pastel Pencils (12-60)—These are harder than soft pastels and, with care, can be sharpened for adding details on eyes, lips, or anything requiring precision. Used lightly, they work well for blending adjacent colors together or creating an overall glazing effect. If you buy a small set, make sure it has light, medium, and dark grays for toning overly bright colors. As with soft pastels, a bigger set will give you a greater range of color expression.

Watercolors—For underpainting large areas, purchase a warm and a cool of the six spectral colors plus a few exotics and earth tones. A good beginning palette includes: cadmium yellow pale, cadmium yellow light, cadmium red light, alizarin crimson, quinacidrone violet (magenta), pthalocyanine purple, ultramarine blue, cerulean blue, manganese blue, viridian green, hookers green deep, yellow ochre, raw sienna, raw umber, burnt sienna, burnt umber, and charcoal gray.

Palette—A good plastic palette with at least 21 wells and, preferably, a cover.

Brushes—Sabeline (synthetic sable) brushes are fine. Try a 1 inch flat and #26 and #12 pointed rounds. Large and small bristle brushes are helpful for scrubbing out small areas.

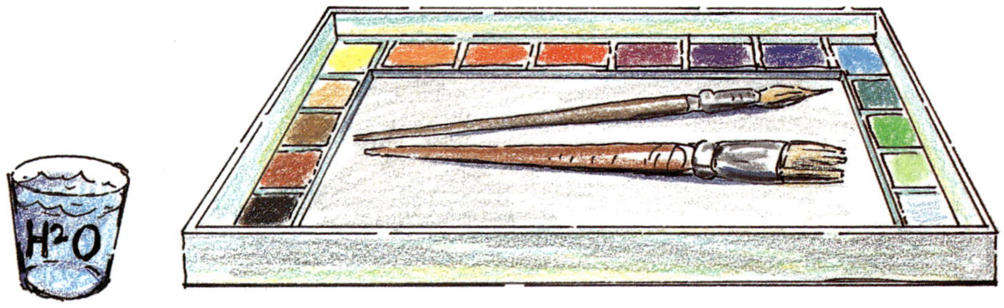

ESSENTIAL SUPPLIES

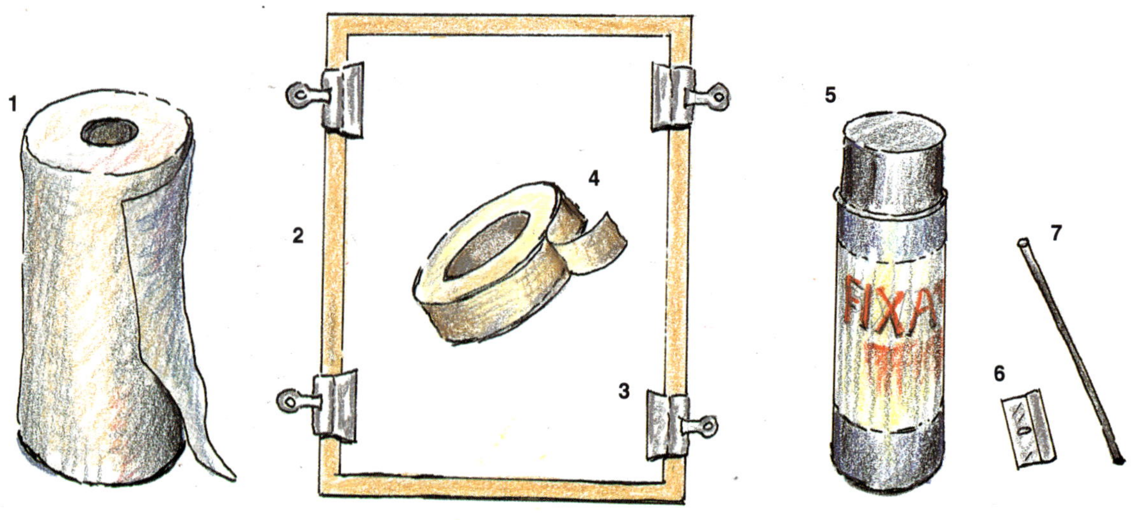

Paper Towels—To clean the chalks as you use them; also good for watercolors.

1/4"Philippine Mahogany Board (watercolor and pastel combined) or **3/16" Foam Core Board** (pastel)—Should be at least 2 inches larger than your paper. Get several so you can work on more than one painting at a time.

Clips—Medium or large; for securing the paper to the board.

Artists' White Masking Tape—This is used in place of clips (if preferred).

Fixative—Useful during the painting process, but rarely at the end.

Razor Blades—For sharpening vine charcoal, pencils, and hard pastels.

Vine Charcoal—Good for initial sketching because it erases easily.

MAKE A PRE-SET FLESH TONE PALETTE • PASTEL SURFACES

Like a tuned piano, ready to play, these chalks are carefully arranged for greater ease in selecting any nuance of white, yellow, red, brown, or black skin color. Take these colors from your large set of soft pastels, or buy them as extras. Each of the fifteen colors has three to six matching values of dark through light, and they are arranged in "color family" rows. (More about color on page 10.)

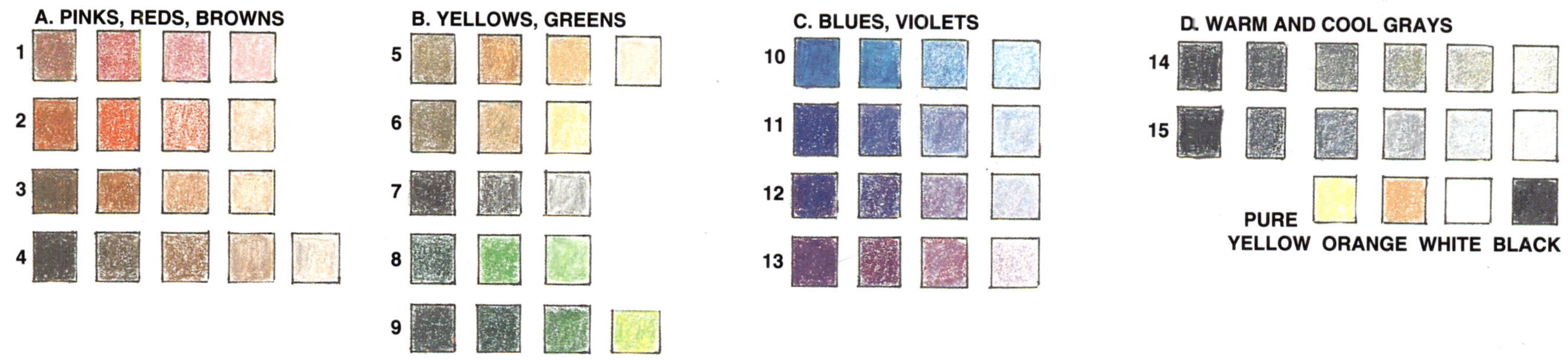

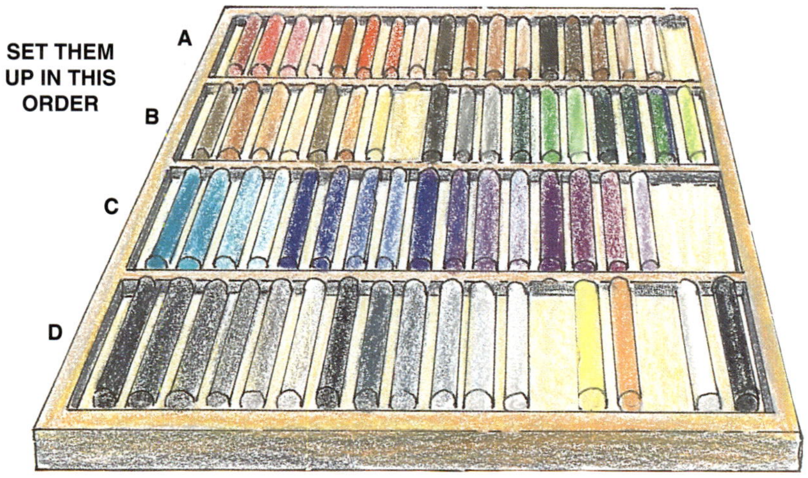

PRE-SET PASTEL COLORS

Row A: 1. Carmine, 2. Permanent Red, 3. Burnt Sienna, 4. Burnt Umber.

Row B: 5. Gold Ochre, 6. Raw Sienna, 7. Raw Umber, 8. Permanent Green, 9. Olive Green.

Row C: 10. Turquoise Blue, 11. Ultramarine Blue, 12. Blue-violet, 13. Red-violet.

Row D: 14. Warm Grays, 15. Cool Grays, 16. Pure Yellow, Pure Orange, White, and Black.

You can see by this selection of colors that "flesh" is really quite grayish. Pure orange and yellow are exceptions; they are used to brighten dulled-out reds and ochres. Greens, blues, and violets are useful for cooling and enlivening through contrast, while grays are helpful for massing in shadows and neutralizing overly active areas.

PRE-SET PASTEL PENCILS

This selection matches the grays, pinks, reds, and ochres of the pre-set pastel set. These pencils are very useful toward the end of a painting for adding details on eyes, nostrils, lips, and ears. A large set of 60 pencils includes these colors, but if you have a small set, I suggest that you buy the ones you're missing by matching the color swatches. These are essential extras. In my own set, the pencils are arranged and numbered, each pencil with its own slot. This makes it easy to keep them in order and to know which colors need replacing.

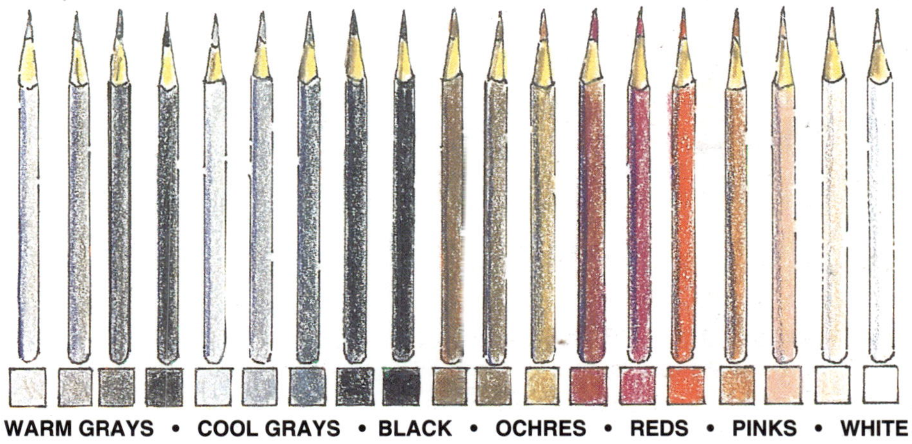

FOUR PASTEL SURFACES

A. Pastel Paper — Light papers are good for accenting darks, medium-value grays are best all around, and dark papers emphasize lights.

B. Watercolor Paper—Use at least a 140 lb., high-quality, cold-press or rough finish.

C. Acid-free Foam Core or Masonite Panel—Either one makes a good support. The masonite is stronger, but heavier; the foam core is a lightweight alternative.

D. Mounted or Stretched Canvas or Linen—Fabrics can be mounted onto a masonite panel with white glue or stretched and stapled onto wooden stretcher bars.

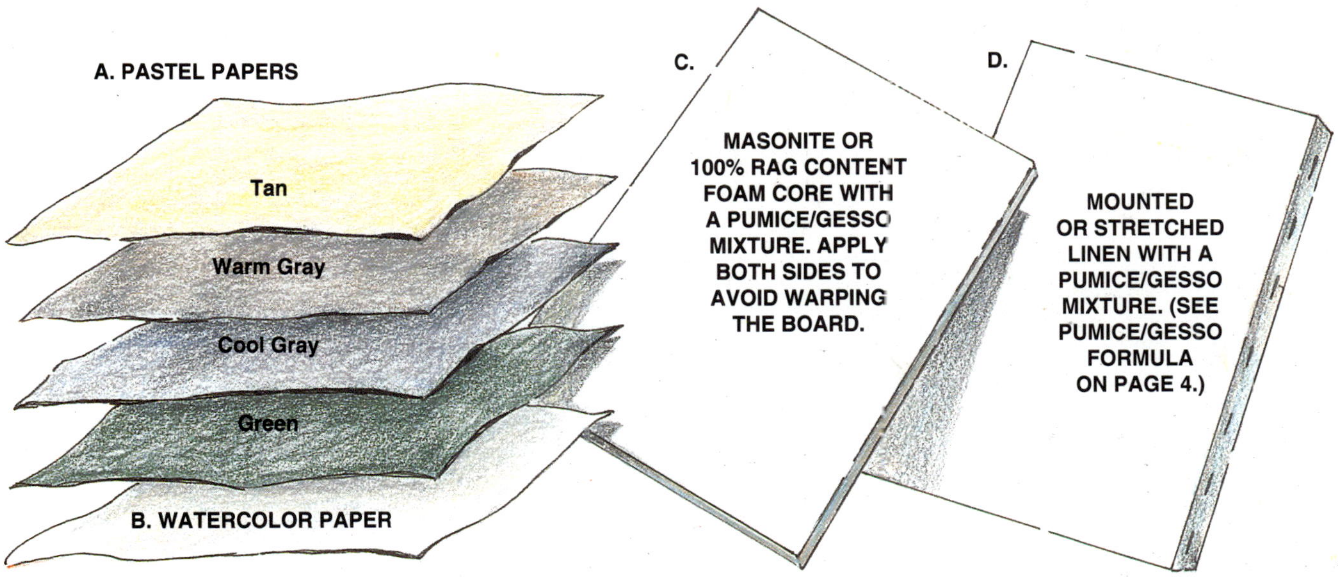

All pastel grounds require "tooth" (texture). On a smooth surface, the texture is filled in quickly, whereas a rougher surface takes longer. When the surface won't accept any more pigment, brush off the excess with a stiff brush, or spray it with a workable fixative. Use pumice/gesso on panels and fabrics (see page 4).

PREPARING YOUR PAINTING SURFACE

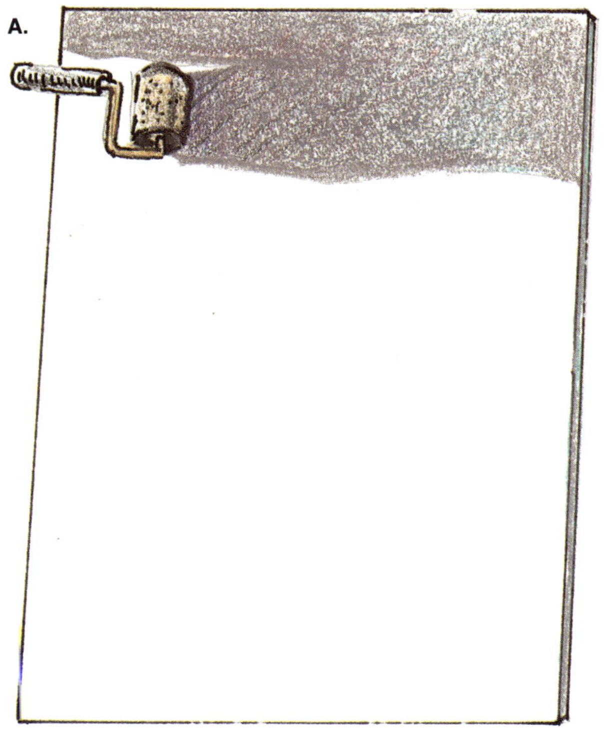

PUMICE/GESSO FORMULA
(Makes one cup)

1. Mix 1/2 cup gesso and 1/2 cup water in a plastic container.
2. Add 4 level tablespoons of medium or coarse pumice to the mixture. Put a lid on the container and shake well. The consistency should be like thick cream.
3. (Optional) For a toned ground, add acrylic paint (black or earth tones work well).

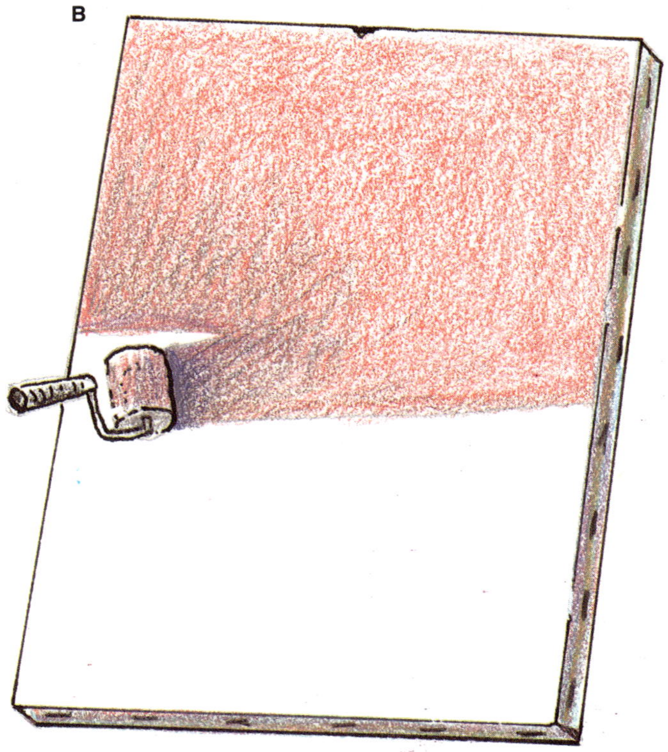

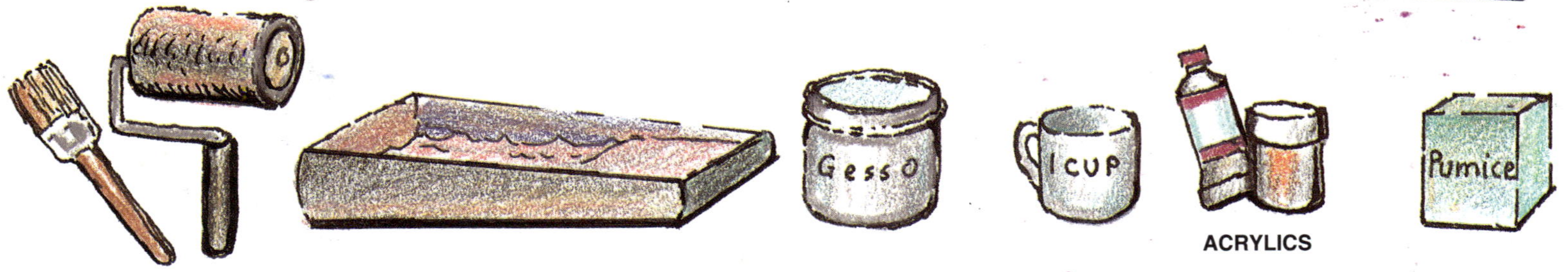

A. Foam Core—To prime acid-free foam core board, (1) put the mixture into a rolling pan; (2) lean the board against a wall; (3) roll or brush on the mixture; (4) quickly turn the board around and repeat the procedure on the back side (one coat per side is adequate). With both sides coated, warping should be minimal.

B. Cotton or Linen—Stretch your own fabric or buy a ready-made canvas (18 x 24 inches is a good size to begin with). Lay the canvas flat and apply one coat gesso/pumice mixture. Or, if you prefer a raw linen tone, use one coat of transparent acrylic matte medium mixed with pumice.

C. Pastel Paper—Clamp or tape 5 to 10 pieces of pastel paper on a foam core board that is 2 inches wider than the paper size. (The extra padding of paper makes it easier to achieve fine details and broad areas of texture.) The smoother backside of the paper holds pastel well, and its texture is less distracting.

D. Watercolor Paper—Soak 140 lb. cold-press or rough finish paper in water for 3 to 5 minutes, and then lay it flat on a mahogany board and put staples 1/4 inch in from the edge every 1 1/2 inches. At first the paper will look sloppy, but it will dry tight, like a drum. You don't have to stretch the paper if you don't mind a little buckling at the end.

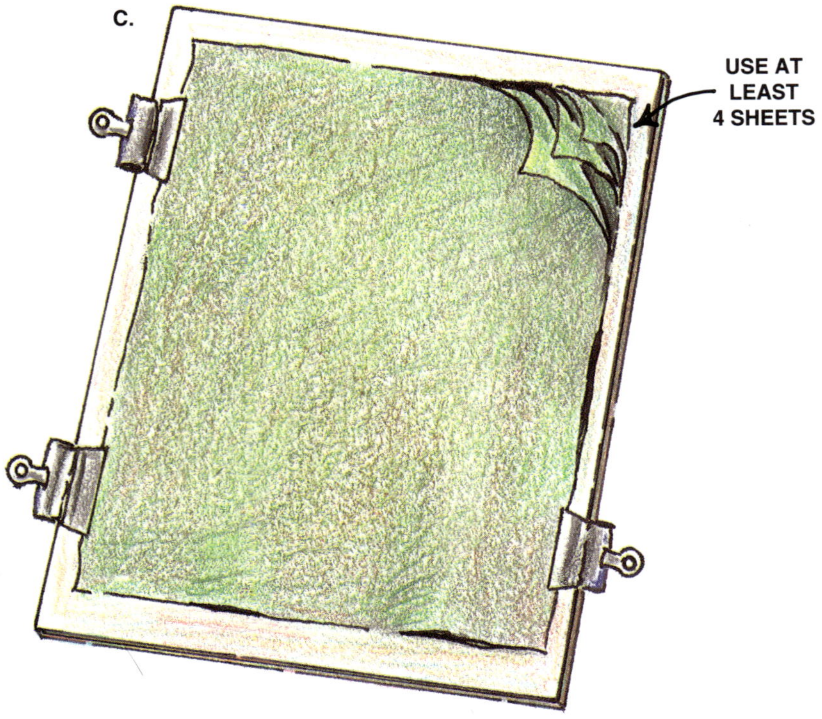

PASTEL STROKES ON FOUR DIFFERENT SURFACES

INTRODUCTION TO PASTEL STROKES

Pastel is a perfect balance between drawing and painting. It can be used in a linear fashion by drawing or crosshatching with the tip, or a half-stick can be used like a brush to lay on wide areas of color. Additionally, by varying the degree of pressure, you can make at least three values from each color. Study the examples at right and the descriptions below to see which names are given to which strokes and how they look on different surfaces.

A. PASTEL PAPER

Feathering can be used for glazing or blending. It is done by delicately stroking an area with pastel pencils or hard pastels. The forehead of this portrait was **feathered** with a gray pastel pencil to tone down the yellows, and the cheeks were **feather-blended** with a light pink. Bright colors successfully **accent** the shadow because when the value is correct, the color can be anything.

B. WATERCOLOR PAPER

Linear crosshatching works especially well over watercolor. Try to make your strokes follow the contours of the facial forms, but don't be too mechanical. Some areas (background and shoulders) work best with vertical strokes, texturizing and revealing existing colors. This technique is known as **"scumbling"** (pigment catches only on the peaks of the paper surface, allowing the valleys to reveal the underpainting). **Scumbling** is an excellent way to enliven dull tones, subdue bright colors, lighten or darken an area, add warmth or coolness, or to blend two forms together.

C. PUMICE/GESSO ON FOAM CORE

Pumice/gesso board can hold a lot of pastel and offers a wide range of textural possibilities. Notice how the background **linear scumbled strokes** look grainy compared to the face, which has been **blended**. A finger was used to blend the forehead and right cheek, and a pastel pencil with **feathered strokes** was used for the left cheek. Part of the neck and collar is partially hatched and part is left alone. Notice how the background colors—gray, green, pink, and yellow—are applied in a scrawled manner so that a little of each color shows through. This sparkling textural effect makes a good contrast for the smoother face.

D. PUMICE/GESSO ON STRETCHED CANVAS

Pastel can be applied on raw canvas, but one good tap on a heavily pasteled area can dislodge all your efforts and make the dust fly. The extra tooth afforded by pumice makes a big difference in holding power and is well worth the extra time! Notice the **scumbled** areas of orange and turquoise behind the head. These areas add textural interest to the large, flat pink background. Also, see how the webbed canvas surface is evident throughout, regardless of the type of strokes used.

A. Pastel Paper

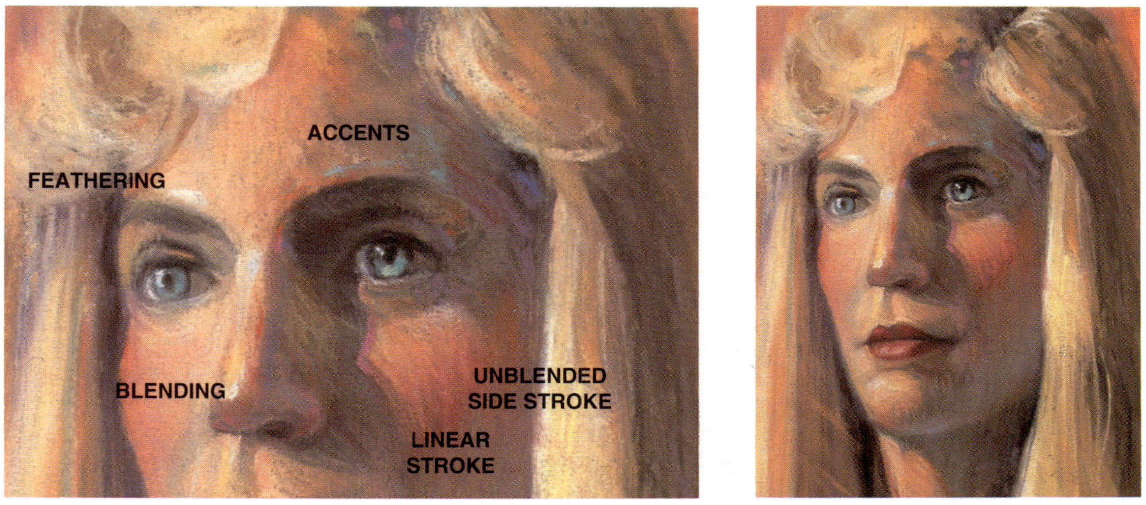

B. Watercolor Paper

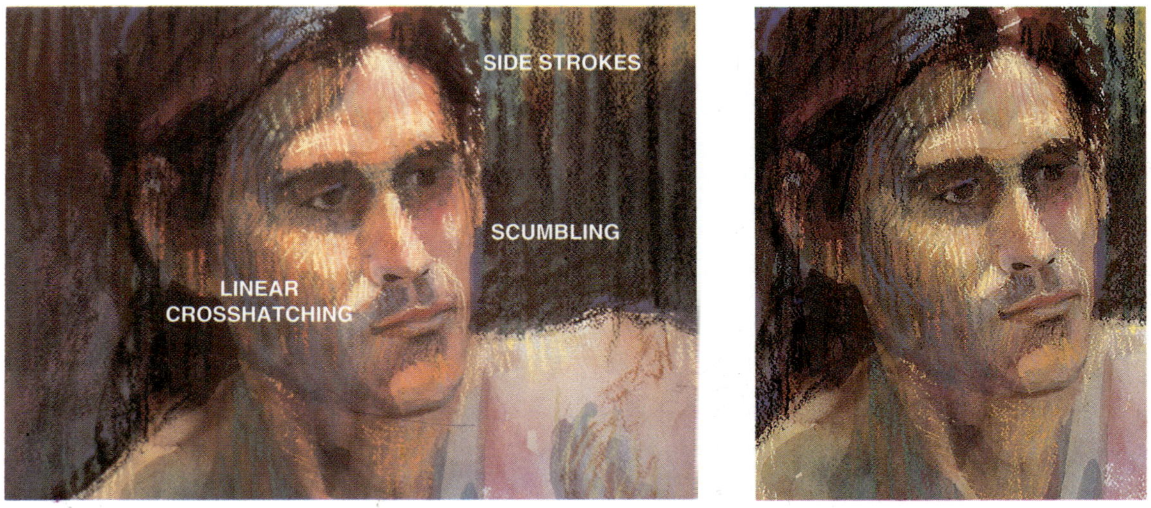

C. Pumice/Gesso On Foam Core

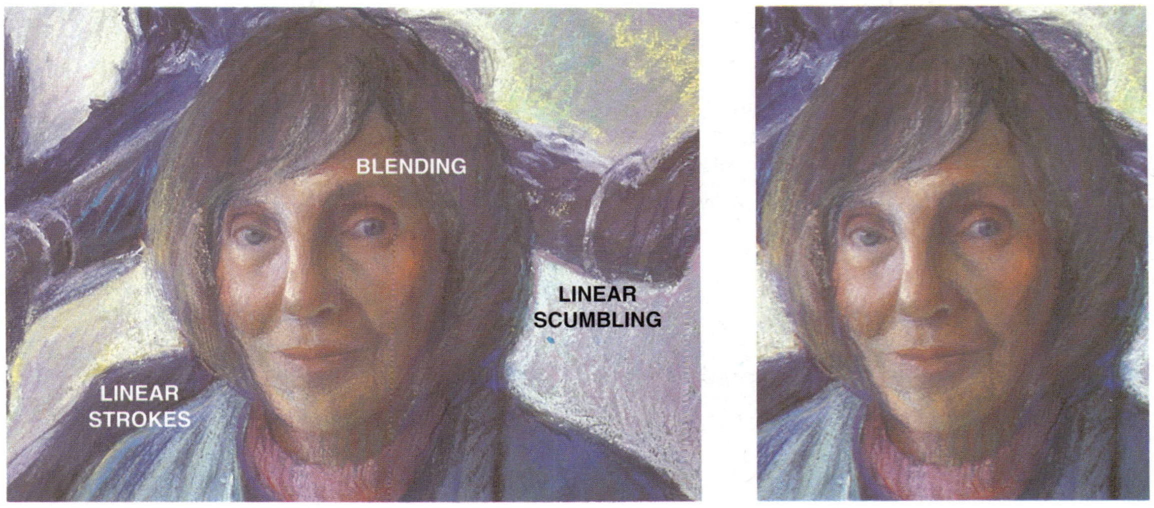

D. Pumice/Gesso On Stretched Canvas

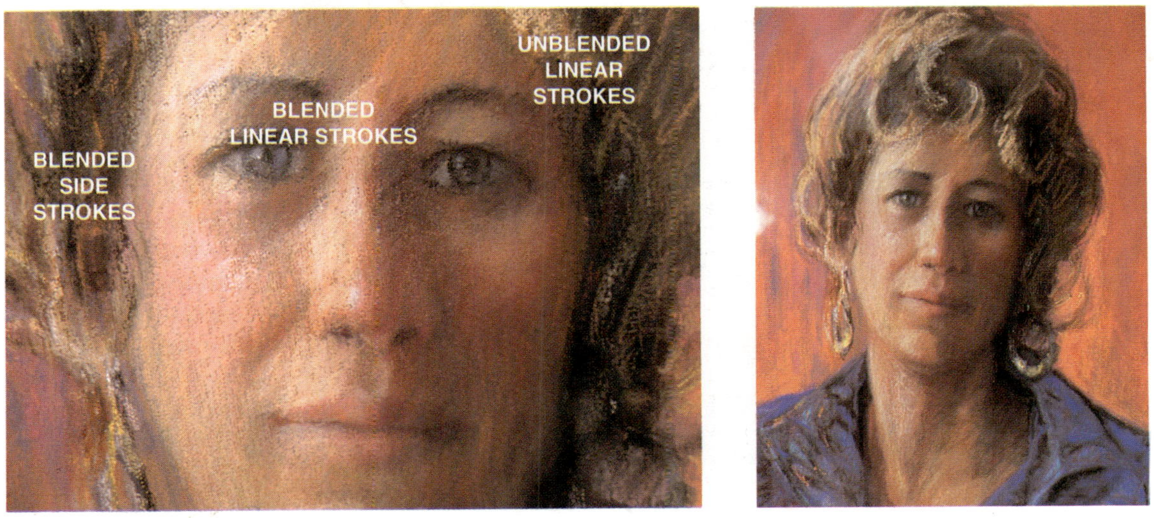

STUDIO ARRANGEMENTS

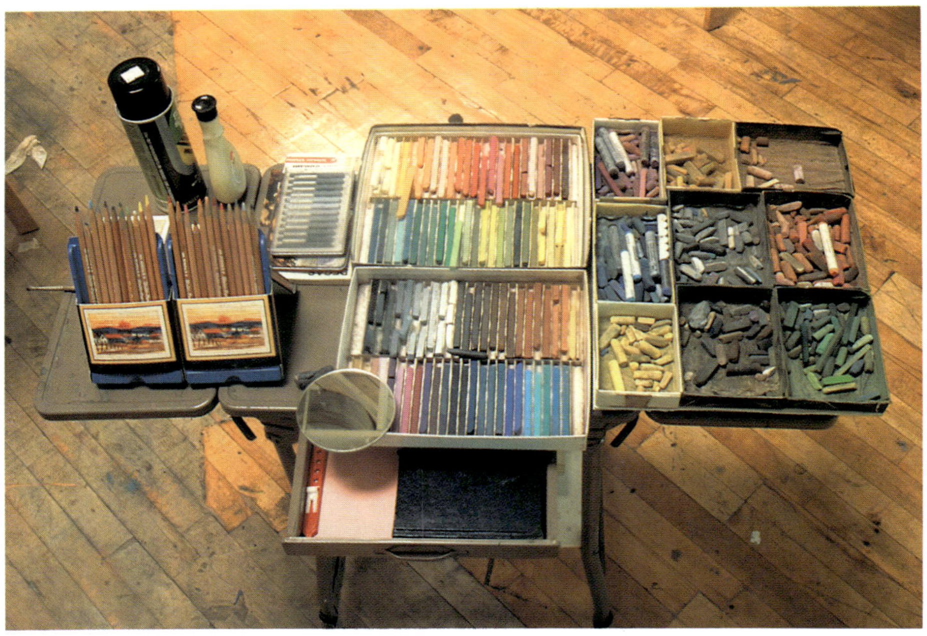

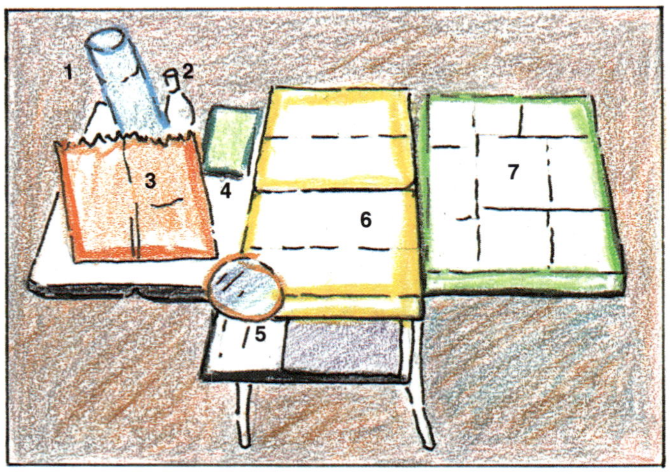

A typewriter stand (new or used) makes a good taboret. Setup: (1) fixative, (2) hand lotion, (3) pastel pencils (small set), (4) set of gray pastels, (5) hand mirror, (6) hard pastels, (7) soft pastels (grouped into color families).

When working on a portrait, you don't want to be troubled by disarray, and, like a pilot in a cockpit, whatever you need for painting should be within easy reach. If you're right-handed, keep your most important supplies to the right and on the easel in front of you. Try using a mirror throughout the painting process for checking the pose compared to your work. This reversed image continually offers a fresh perspective. If you have a skylight or window, it's good to eliminate other light sources; if you use artificial light, use balanced-spectrum fluorescent bulbs above your easel and a spotlight on a variable-height light stand for the model. A one-foot model stand is helpful for raising the model closer to your eye level.

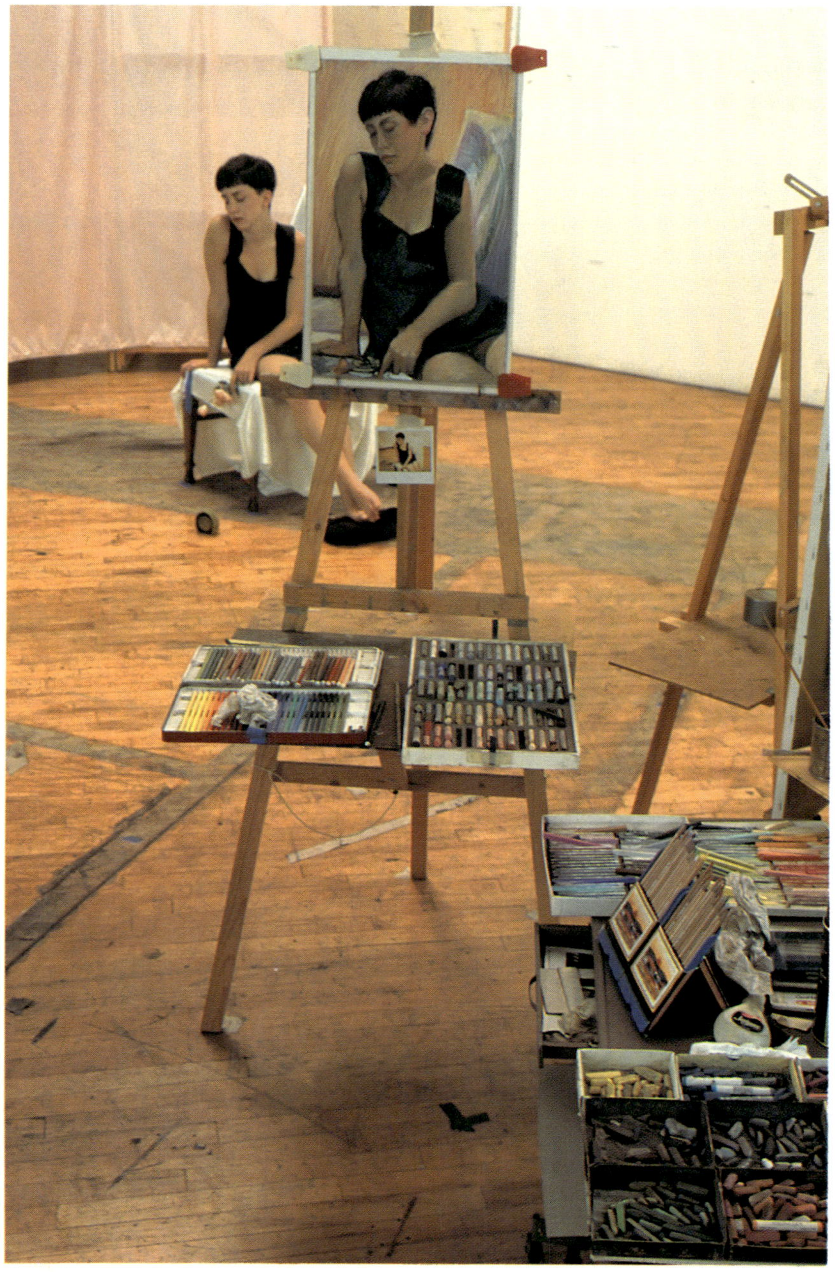

Setup for a skylit studio.

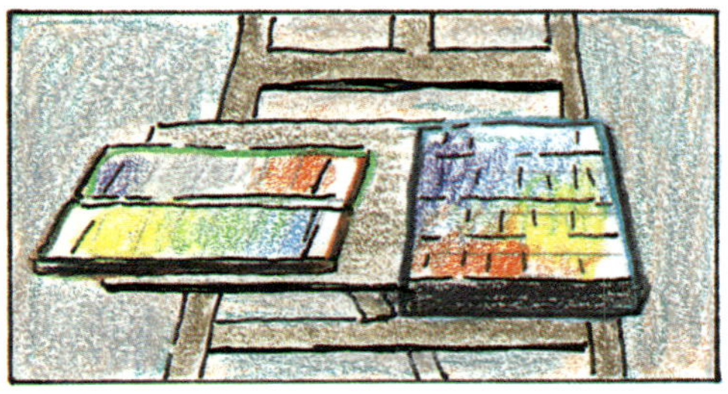

The easel shelf is used for the large set of pastel pencils (1) and the pre-set flesh tones (2).

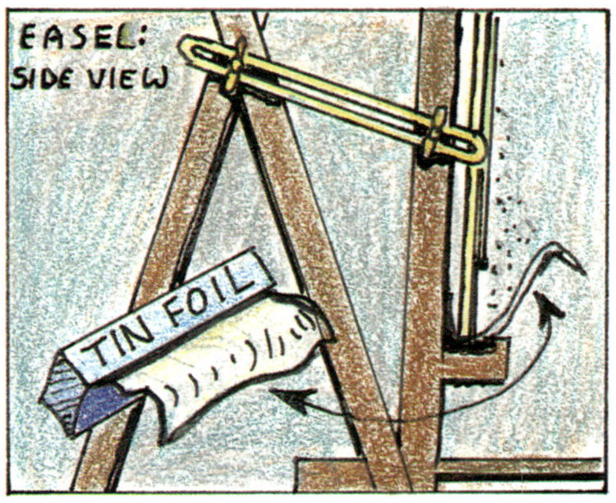

It is helpful if your easel can tilt forward slightly. This allows the pastel dust to bypass your art as it falls, which helps to keep your work cleaner. A folded piece of aluminum foil placed under the board makes an excellent gutter for catching the dust.

The photo at left shows how the setup might look during a portrait session. If you are right-handed, it is easier to look over your left shoulder. Notice the Polaroid snapshot under the painting. Polaroids are helpful if the model drifts in and out of position. This portrait is being done under a diffused skylight, 30 feet high. If you are a beginner, a spotlight is recommended because the strong contrasts help reveal the forms of the model. When you use a spotlight, it is best to darken other light sources.

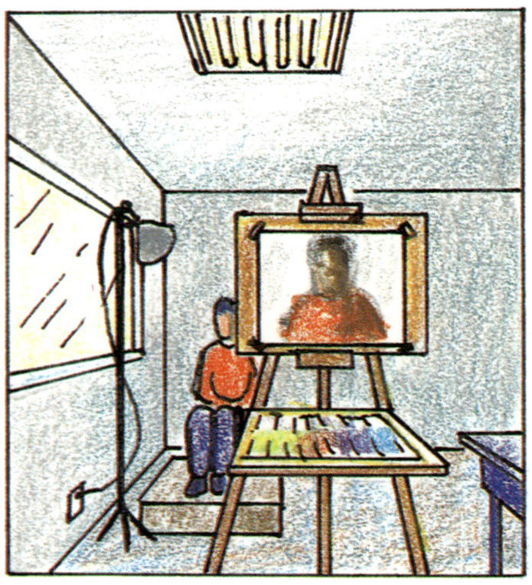

Right-handed Setup—To avoid casting a shadow on your work, the lights should come from above and the left. (The reverse is true for a left-handed setup.)

PAINTING FROM A LIVE MODEL AND SETTING THE POSE

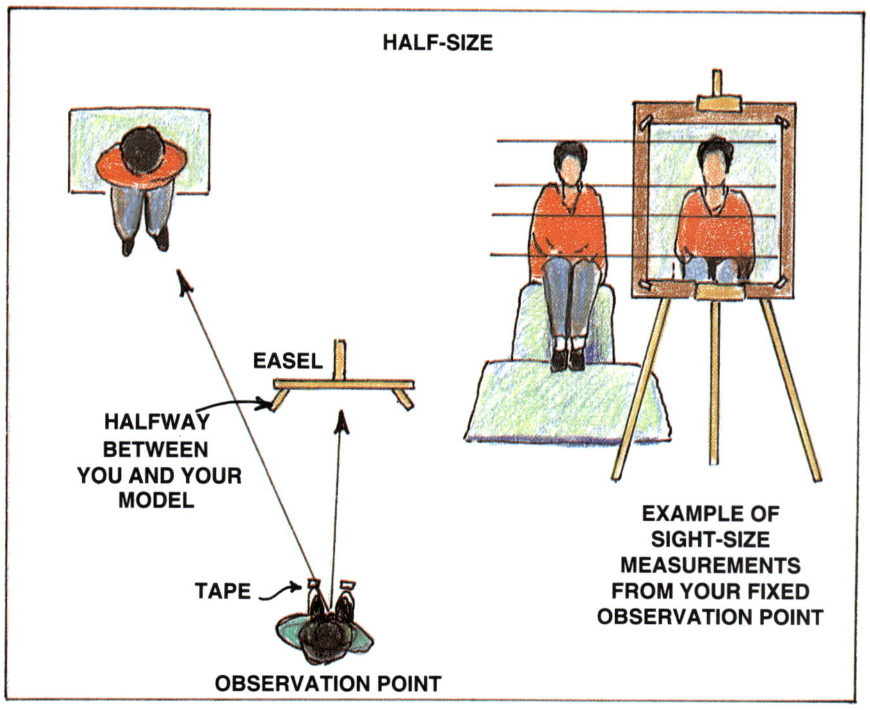

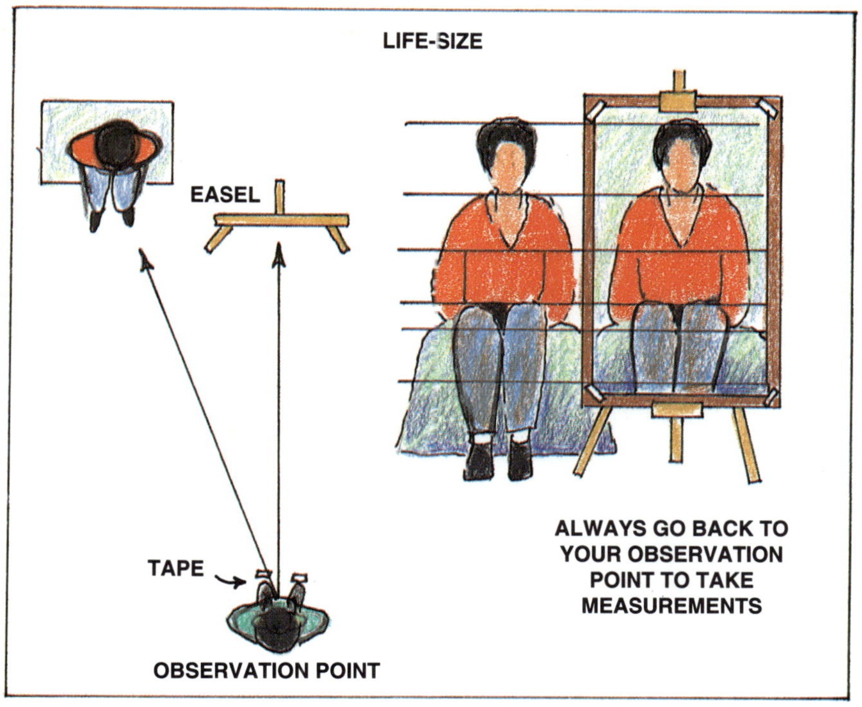

Painting "Sight-Size"—After you have set your model and chosen an observation point, position your easel so the *drawing measurements* on your paper will be the *same size as what you see* ("sight-size"). Make all your decisions about the painting from this point, because if you make decisions from any other position, everything will change. Unlike landscape painting, portraiture is dependent on a stationary viewpoint, and you might even want to go so far as to put tape marks on your viewing spot. Each stroke requires a walk to your easel and back again to your observation point. It is very tempting to be lazy and look while you're at the easel, but try not to. The only justification for observing from your easel would be if that was where you started and that was your observation point. Most people paint close to their easels, and you might find this easier at first, especially if you're working fairly small. However, in the long run it is better to get used to painting from a distance and developing your visual memory. The two diagrams above show a "sight-size" setup for both half-size and life-size portraits.

PAINTING FROM PRINTS AND SLIDES AND REAR-SCREEN PROJECTORS

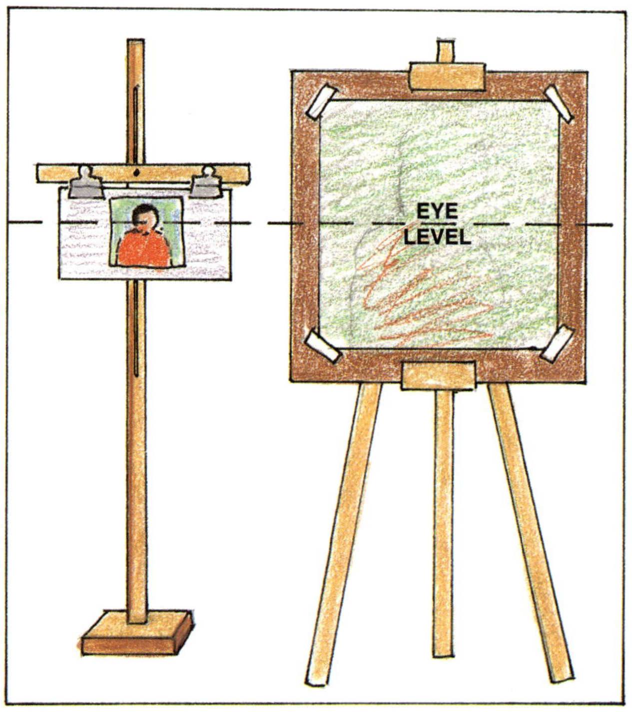

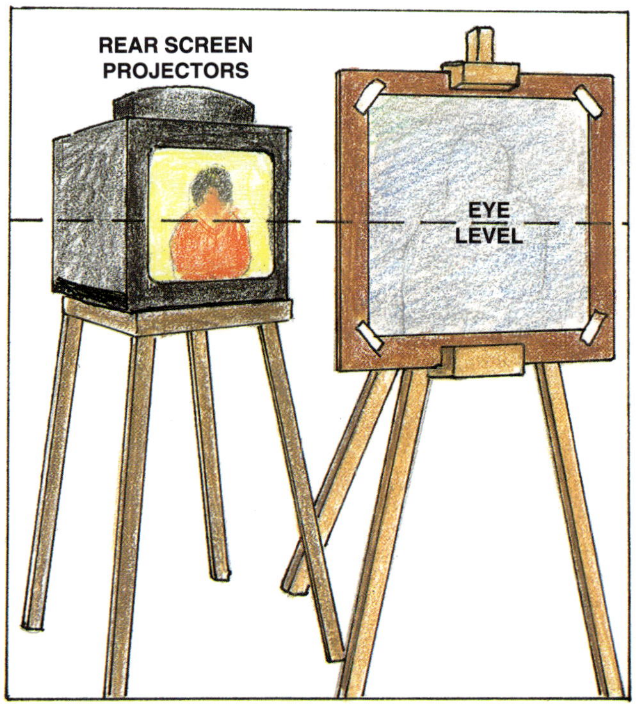

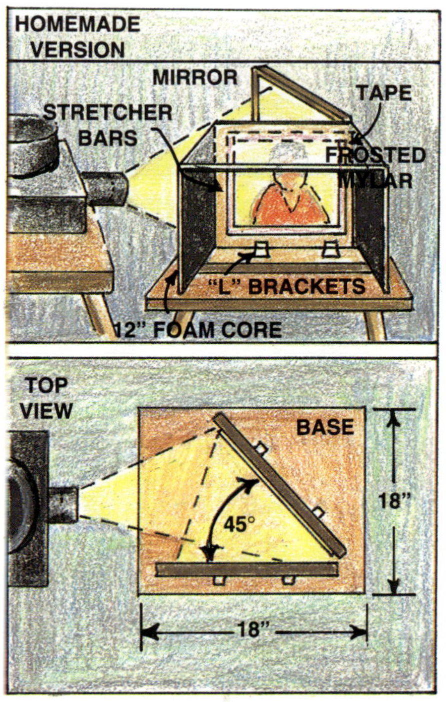

If your studio isn't large enough for a model stand, or if you want to work on your live portraits between sessions, prints and slides are a great help. They are also invaluable for doing children, pets, complicated group portraits, or simply for practicing. However, when you use them, remember that the camera "lies." Values are usually too dark in the shadows and too light in the lights, and the lens can often make subtle distortions. If you are well-versed in painting from life, you can compensate for these distortions. If not, you should join a local life drawing group or paint self-portraits or still lifes, etc. Then try working from photos as if they, too, had three dimensions. The diagrams above show methods of working from prints or slides. To keep the images at eye level, the cross bar for prints is adjustable, and the projector stand is built just under eye level. For slides, you can use a rear-screen projector, or, if you can't find one and already have a regular projector, follow the plans for making your own. A note about these plans: When you tape the frosted mylar onto the stretcher bars, face the shiny side in. (The 45° angled mirror is for reducing lamp glare.)

COMPOSING YOUR PORTRAIT

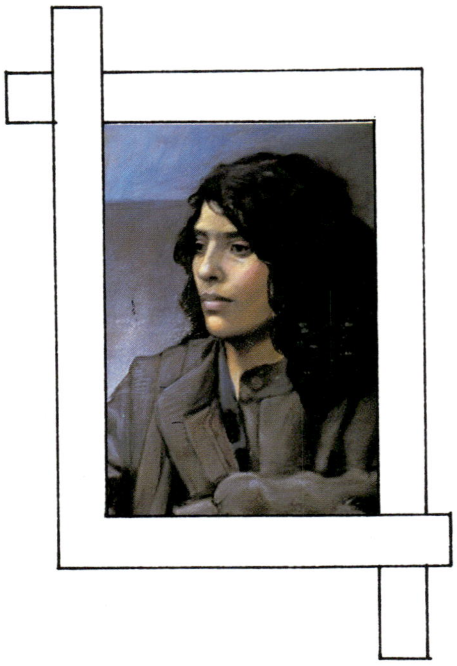

This portrait is composed poorly. The face feels cramped to the left edge, and the hair does not provide enough interest to warrant extra space.

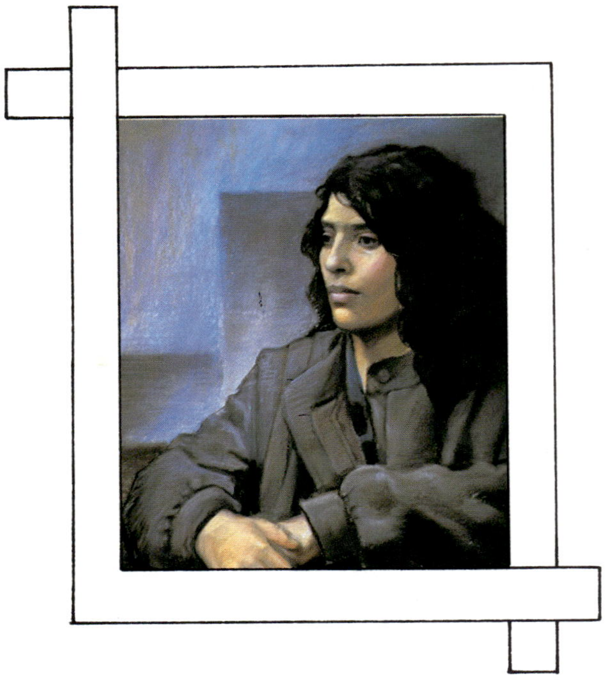

This composition is better as far as the head placement is concerned, but now the arms are cropped at an awkward place.

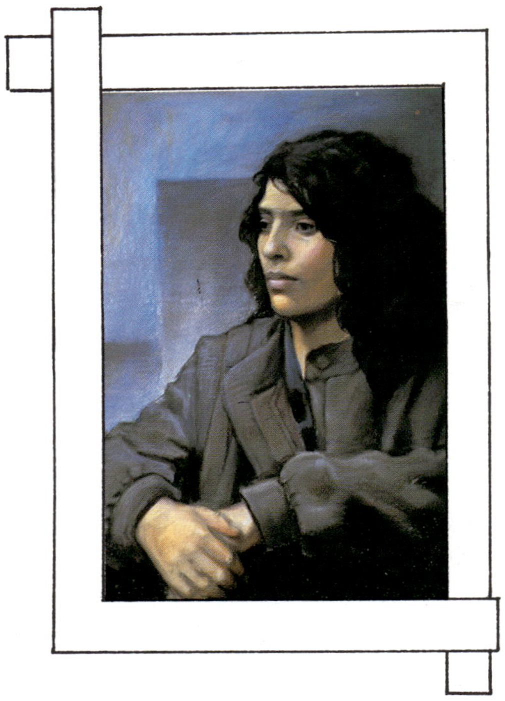

This vertical composition would work only if the background horizontals could have been included to repeat the horizontal arm. There is no stability to the strong up-and-down movement.

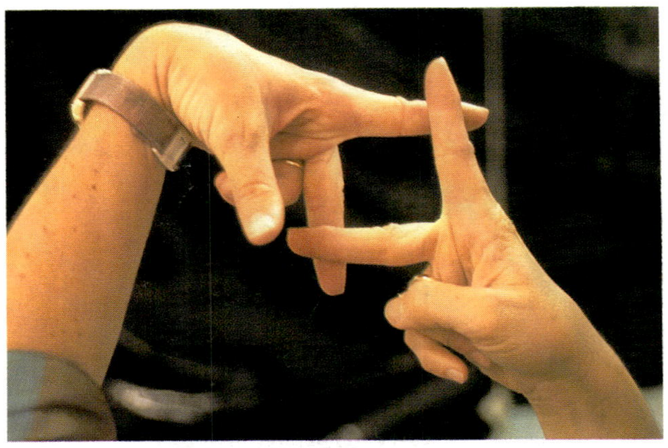

COMPOSITION

Composition refers to the placement of shapes or forms within a painting. These shapes—head, figure, and background—must please and excite the eye of the viewer, or the viewer will simply find something else to look at. Before you start working on your portrait, make a double "L" with your fingers (make it the same proportions as your paper) or make a cardboard viewfinder and check your composition by looking through the opening. While moving your hands or viewfinder away from your face, the figure will fill more of the frame; by bringing them closer, the figure gets smaller. One composition deals with a closeup of the model while the other deals with a figure in space. Some basic rules to follow when composing a portrait are to make each of the four quarters of your paper different, to look for asymmetry whenever possible, and, most importantly, to pick one of the countless possibilities that excites you and get started. In contrast to the examples above, the composition to the right seems to work best.

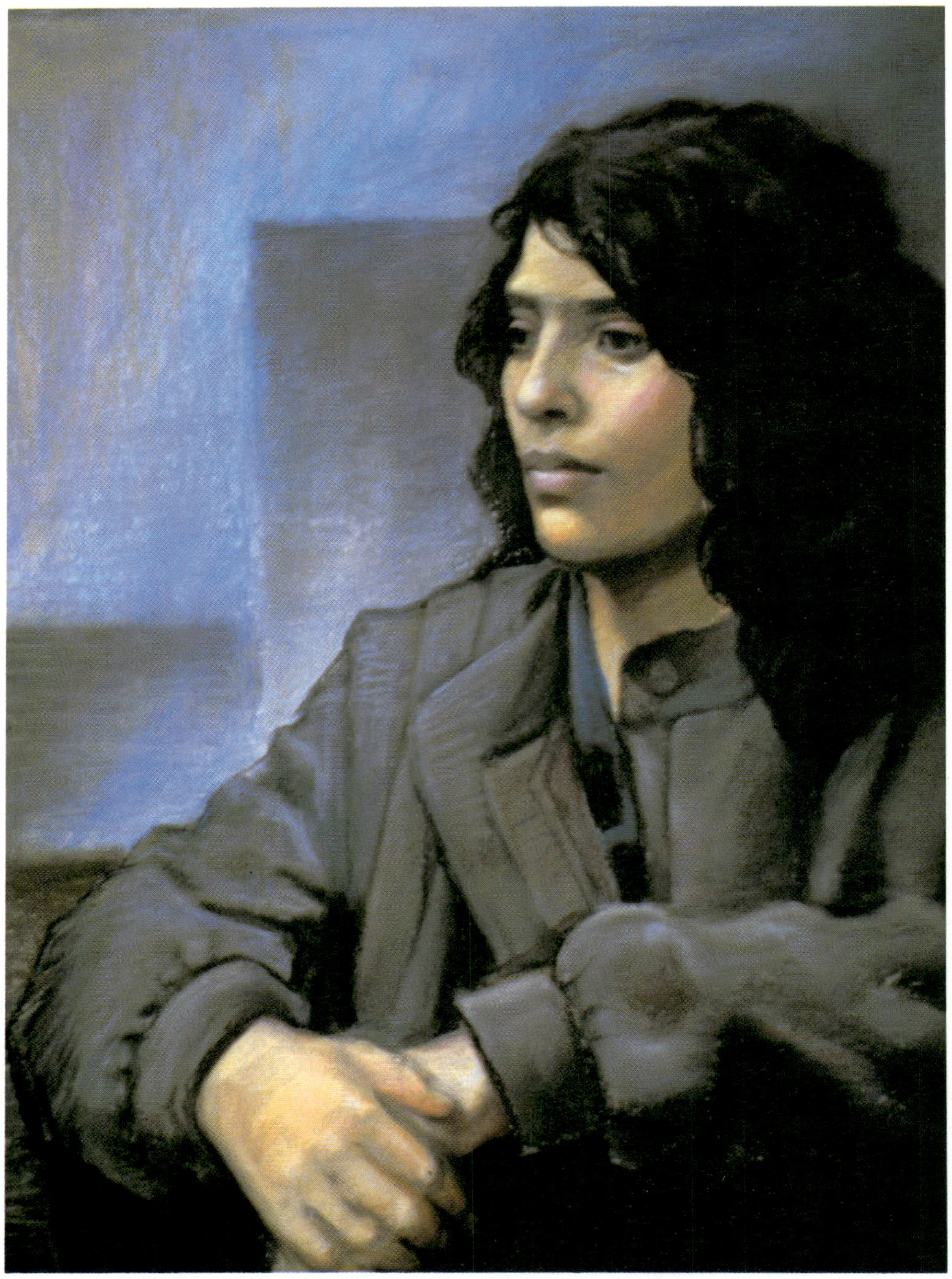

COMPOSITIONAL DYNAMICS AND PAINTING REFLECTIONS

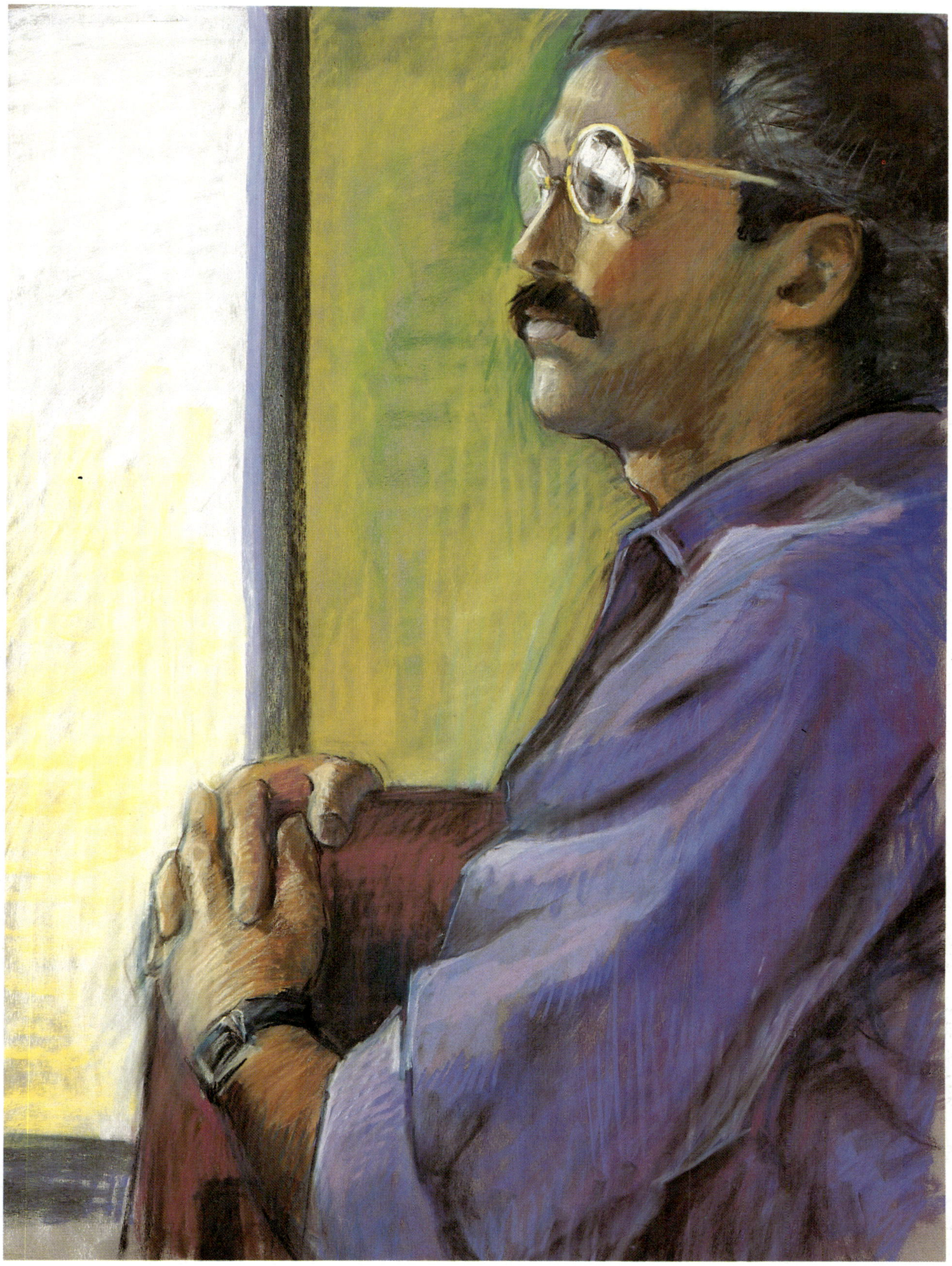

Rick Pastel On Pumice Board 26 x 20

When composing a portrait, pay special attention to "visual flow." The odd cropping of this portrait catches the eye—the diagonal arm leads the eye in while the verticals and horizontals keep the eye moving. Some principles of design for this portrait are described briefly below.

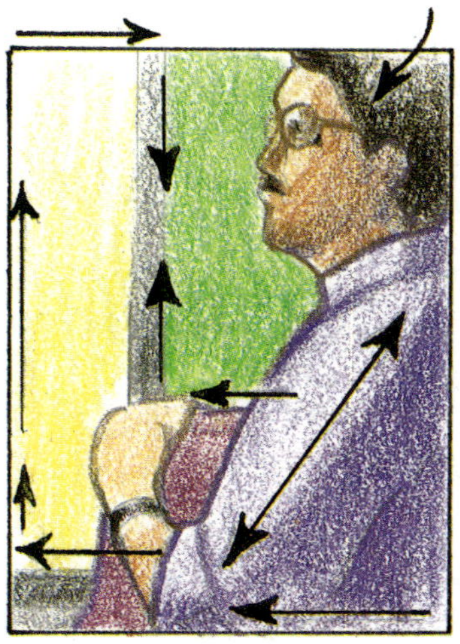

The eye is activated by **movement**. In this composition, movement is created with **contrast**, **dominance**, **repetition**, and **gradation**. For **contrast** there are dark areas against light, large shapes against small, and thick lines against thin; for **dominance** there are more darks than lights and more vertical emphasis than horizontal; for **repetition** the horizontal eyeglass frame repeats with the chair and window base, and the oval glasses repeat with the ear; for **gradation** the arm creates a gradual diagonal from vertical to horizontal and the four main values from dark to light.

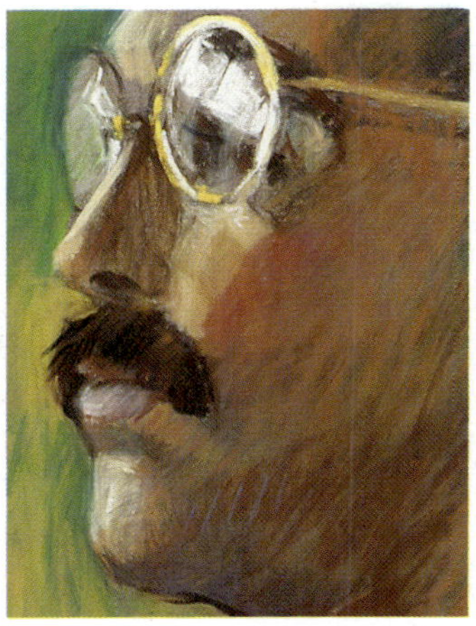

Painting an eye behind eyeglasses is one of the few times that it is best to forget eye anatomy completely. Behind a lens the eye is usually displaced. You need to paint the distortion accurately for it to appear realistic. Squint your eyes when you look, then paint the **shapes** as you see them with attention to correct values. The end result will be better than if you try to paint the eye first and then the glasses.

COLOR WHEEL BASICS

The purpose of this page is to simplify and clarify terms that a painter should know when analyzing a model and selecting colors to use. All the confusing brand names such as Avocado, Mauve, Taupe, etc., can be called out as members of the twelve spectral colors on this wheel and described by the six color terms on this page (this will be discussed later).

Red, yellow, and blue are called "primary" because they cannot be obtained by mixing any other colors. When all three primaries are combined in equal proportions, the result is neutral gray (see #1). Orange, violet, and green are mixed from two primaries, so they are called "secondaries." Intermediates of yellow-orange, red-orange, red-violet, blue-violet, blue-green, and yellow-green are often called "tertiary" because they are the third result of mixing a primary and secondary together. If you make a color wheel like this one, be sure each primary is a true primary; for example, red must be pure; it can't lean towards violet or orange. Secondaries should also be true; for example, orange shouldn't lean toward red or yellow. The same is true with the intermediates. Also, take note that every color on either side of the wheel gets progressively darker in value from yellow, which is lightest, to violet, which is darkest (see #1 and #4).

COLOR TERMS

Hue—The name of a color: red, yellow, green, etc. (see #1).

Value—The lightness or darkness of a color, usually given an ascending number from 1 to 9 (see #2).

Chroma—The purity or strength of a color (see #3), ranging from intense (high) to neutral (low). At a definite value, each color has a point of highest chroma, or intensity (see #4); i.e., red is most saturated at value #6, yellow at value #2, etc. (Neither #1 nor #9 is ever considered intense in any color, so they are not even included.) Any change from a high chroma **value** of color up or down the scale will automatically weaken the chroma (see #5).

Temperature—On the color wheel (see #1), the red side is considered warm, the blue side cool. Red-orange is often considered warmest, blue-green coolest. However, this is relative; any warm color can be cool and vice versa depending on what it is next to; i.e., blue-violet is cool compared to any red, but it is warm compared to blue or blue-green because it is closer to red. Look for other examples.

Tint—Lightening a color by adding white.

Shade—Darkening a color by adding black. A pastel manufacturer lightens or darkens the pure colors in a pastel set by tinting with white or shading with black.

COMPLEMENTARY OPPOSITES

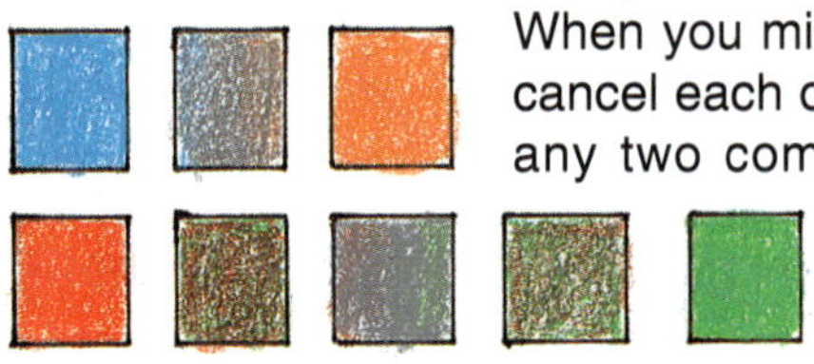

When you mix the three primary colors together, they cancel each other out and make gray (see #1). Mixing any two complements (opposites on the wheel) in equal proportions will also make gray, i.e., red + green = gray. Green is a mixture of blue and yellow, so you are really mixing the three primaries: red, blue, and yellow. Complements visually enliven each other when placed side by side, but they neutralize each other when they are mixed together.

DETERMINING COLORS

Color wheel #6 shows where each of the pure colors in your pre-set flesh tone palette falls on the wheel (other values of the set are not shown here). As in wheel #1, the chroma of colors approaching the center is grayer or browner than at the rim, which is purest. As stated earlier, factory brand names for colors must be translated into names that actually describe the color family you are looking for, i.e., red-orange, blue-green, etc.

There will always be far more colors, values, and chroma variations on your model than you have in your pastel box, and, since you can't copy exactly what you see, you must search for equivalents. To do this, it is helpful to ask yourself certain questions. For example, when you look at a tan sofa, you must forget the name "tan" and ask, "Is this color warm or cool?" You decide it is warm. Now, is it yellowish, or orangey, or what? If it seems sort of yellow, look in the yellow section and ask, "What is its value—light, medium, or dark?" It is light. Is it intense or dull? Fairly dull—it is brownish. This leads you to a light value of raw sienna, which, as you can see on wheel #6, is a dull yellow. Try this method of identification with different objects around you. If a color is too hard to analyze, just call it gray; find the proper value pastel stick; block it in; then come back to the actual color later.

1

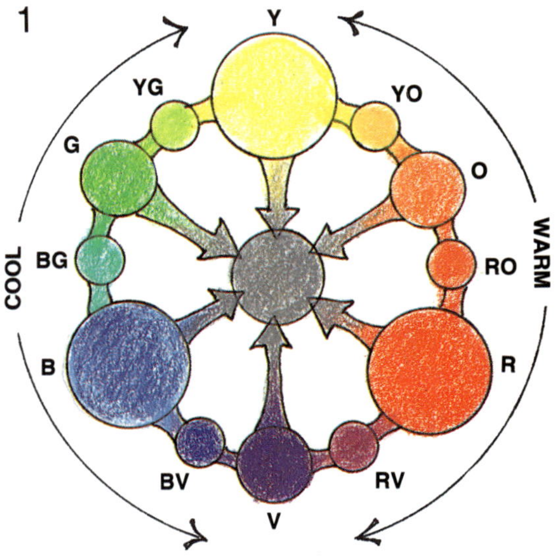

2

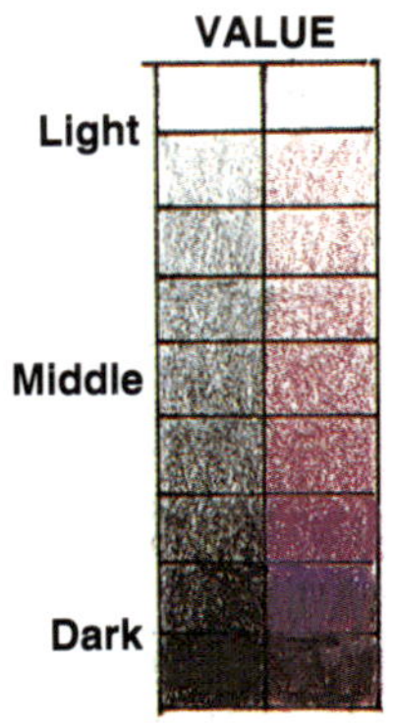

3

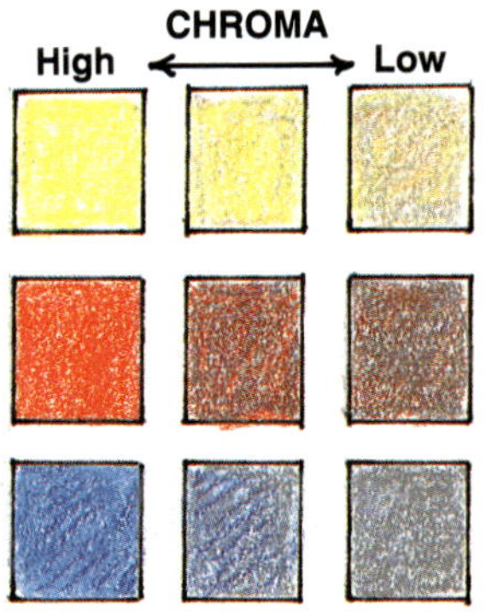

4

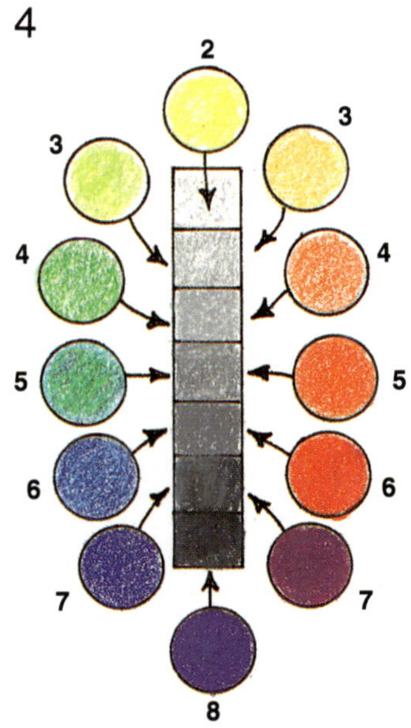

5

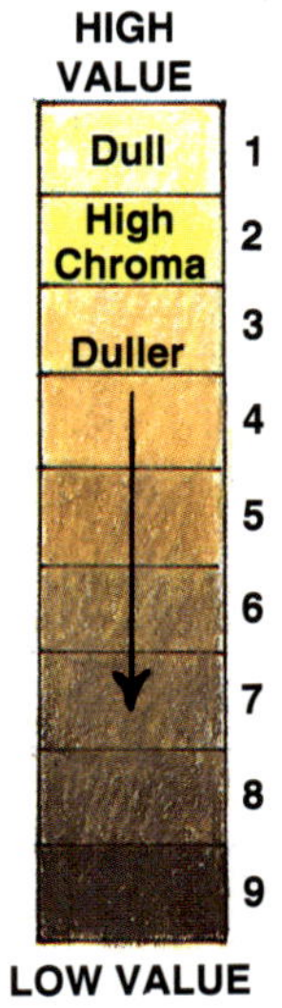

6

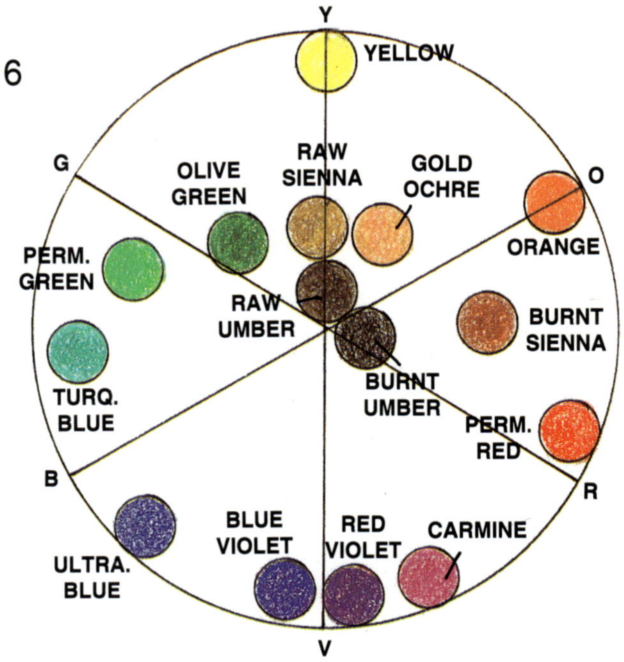

COLOR HARMONIES

Numerous psychological investigations have shown that most people find pleasure in color combinations that are based on either analogy or extreme contrast. Each of these examples is based on different analogous or complementary color schemes; notice how they all convey different moods.

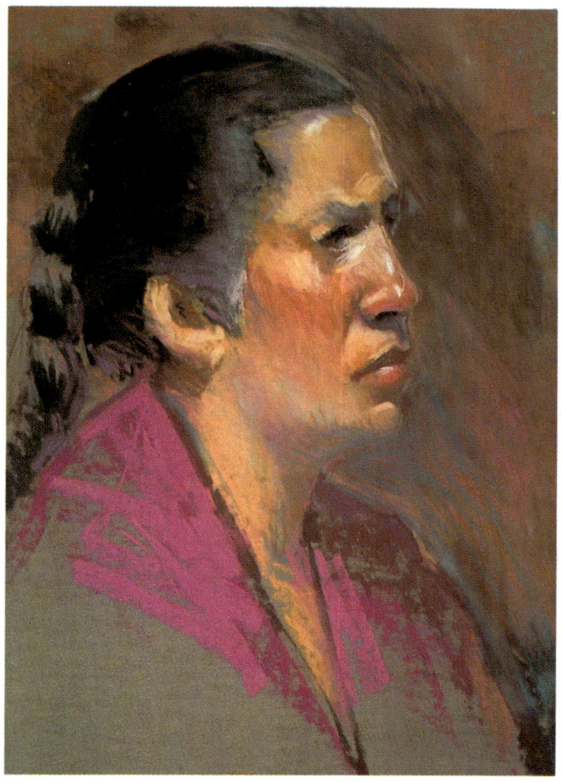

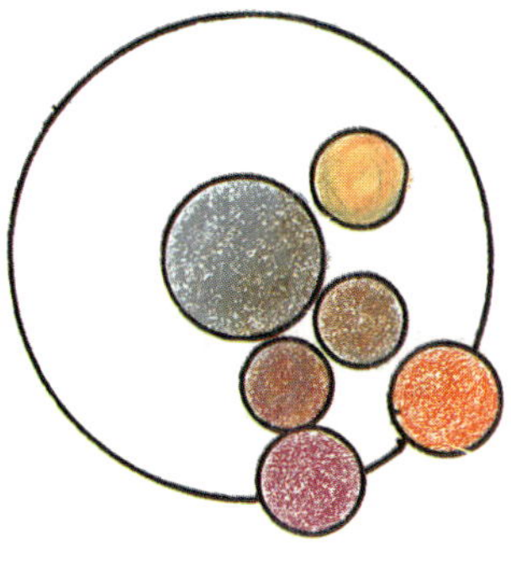

This study of an Indian woman was painted on an umber sanded paper in **analogous** (adjacent), low-chroma brown, red, and yellow-orange tones (with accents of pink and black). The mood is somber because the tones are mostly muted. Notice how the background is subtly grayed with complementary turquoise hatching.

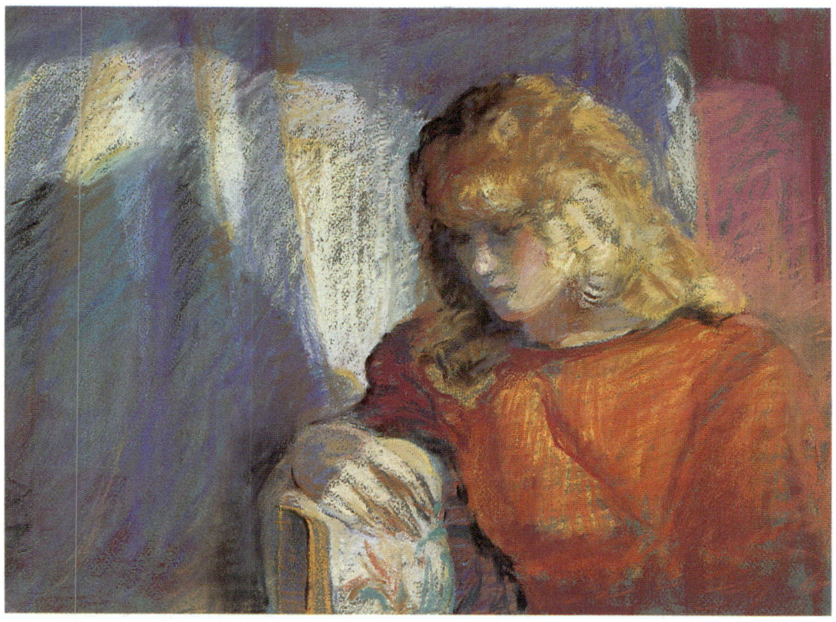

This study is based on a **mutual complementary scheme** in which one color (blue) dominates, and three opposing colors (yellow, orange, purple-red) complement it. Though the sitter seems reflective, the high-keyed colors create an optimistic feeling of light and warmth. Umbers and ochres are feathered into the blue to warm it a bit.

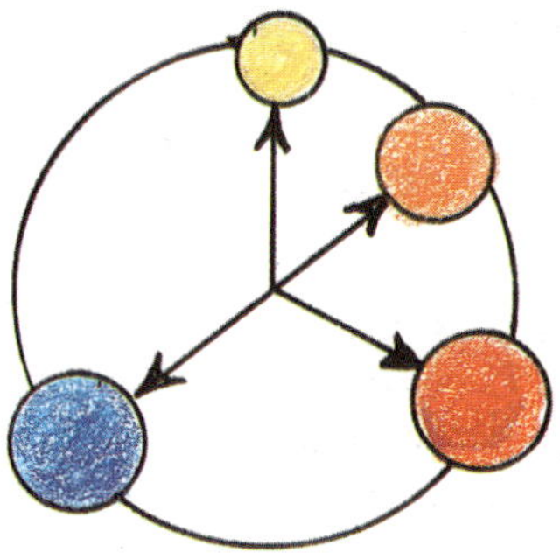

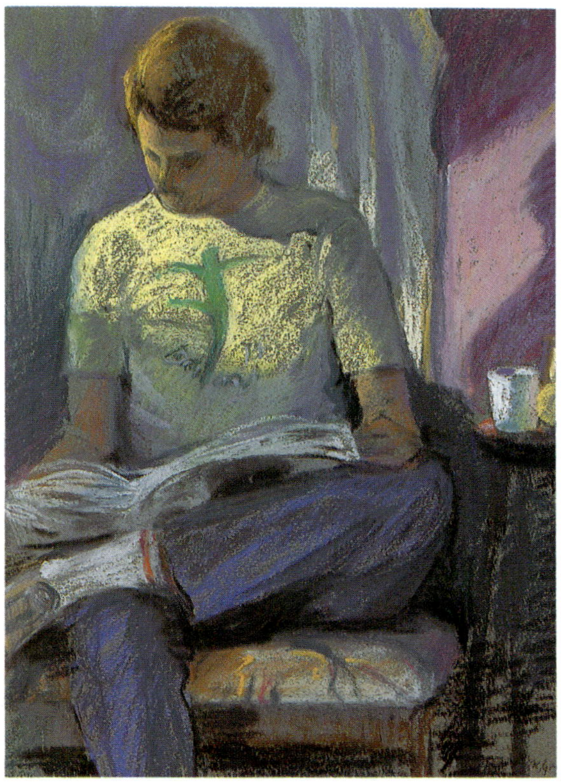

Analogous Harmonies—Analogous color schemes have an emotional quality because they usually give preference to either the warm or cool side of the spectrum. They are useful for inspiring precise moods (i.e., active, passive, somber, etc.), and are easier to use harmoniously than are complementary schemes.

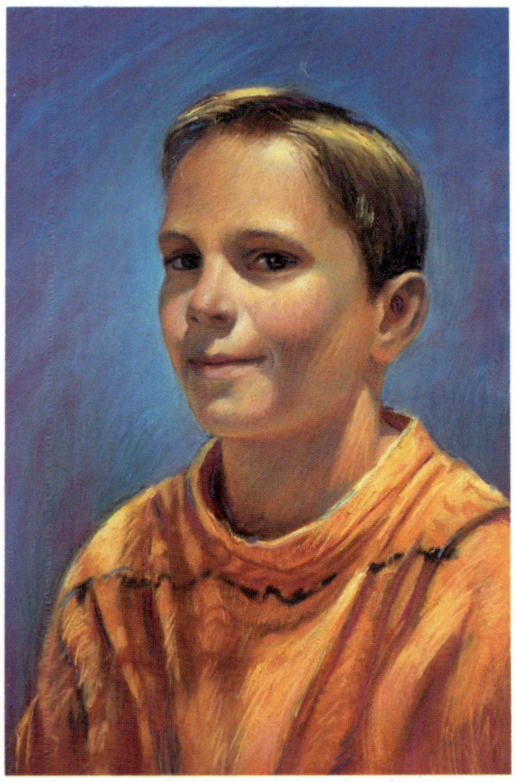

Complementary Harmonies—These color schemes are visually more exciting than analogous color schemes, but they are also less capable of inspiring particular moods. For example, any feeling associated with red or orange, such as warmth, is usually cancelled by the opposite qualities associated with cool green or blue.

Bright colors appear luminous when contrasted to a neutral background, but they appear garish when surrounded by too many other colors. This portrait, which is based on **direct complements** of yellow-green and red-violet, illustrates this point. The eye is excited the contrasting colors, but rested by the neutral ground.

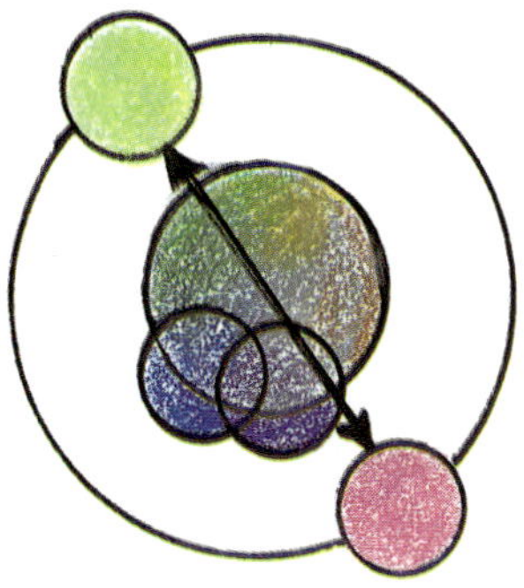

This portrait is based on the **direct complements** of orange and blue. No attempt is made to tone down either color because the extreme contrast conveys a sense of youthful vitality. Since orange is expansive and carries more weight than blue, using an equal amount of both is just as effective as placing a large portion of orange next to a small portion of blue.

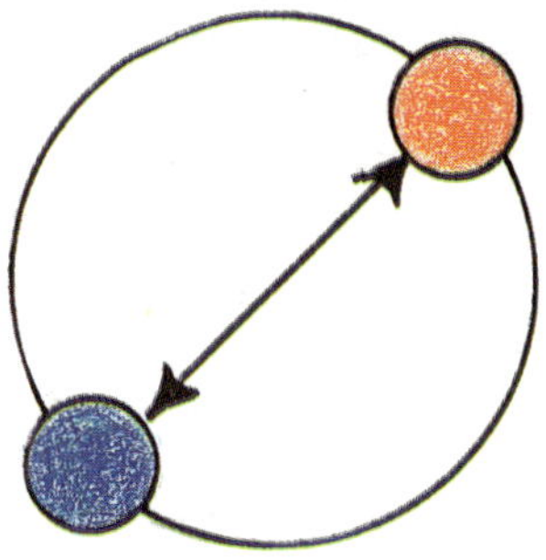

CHOOSING A KEY OF CHROMA AND VALUE

Choice of "key" refers to the general lightness or darkness of a painting and, also, to the overall intensity of color (chroma), which automatically shifts with changes in value (see diagrams). High-key paintings evoke different emotions than low-key paintings, and you should try to know your model well enough to choose the appropriate key at the start.

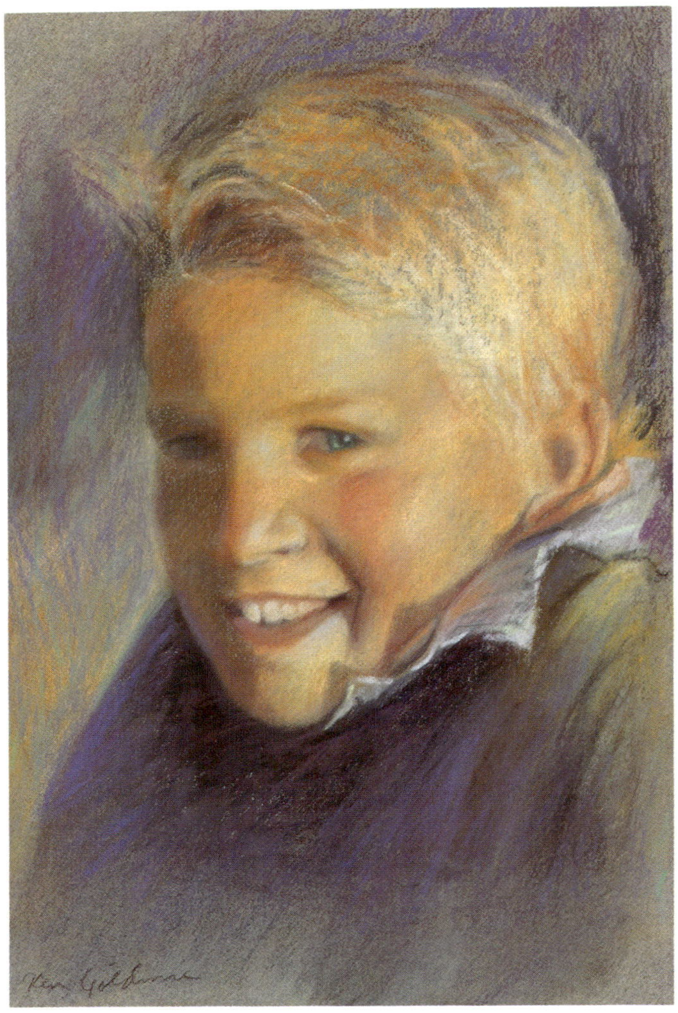

Study For Portrait Of Bron Pastel On Paper 13 x 10

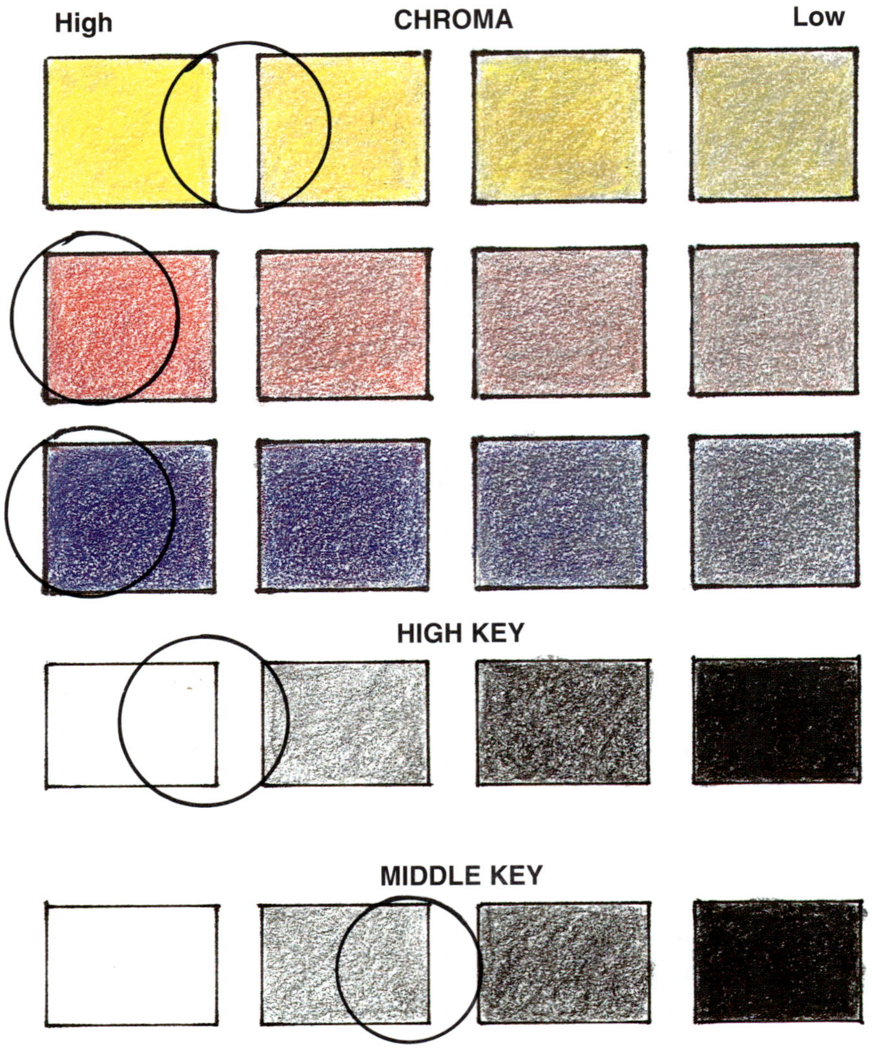

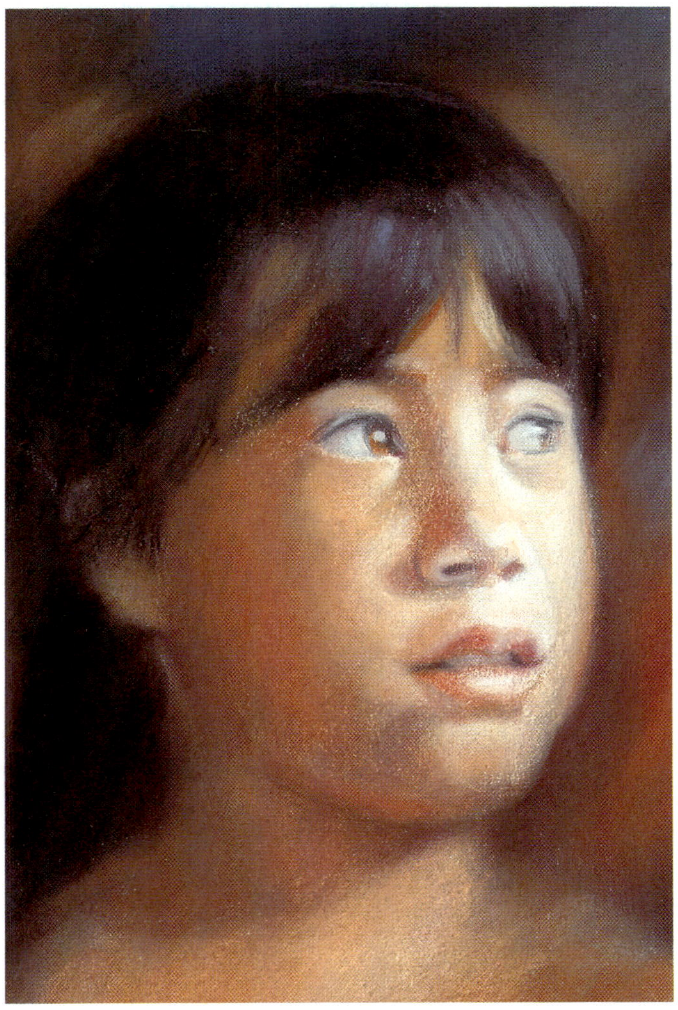

Anela Pastel On Paper 13 x 9

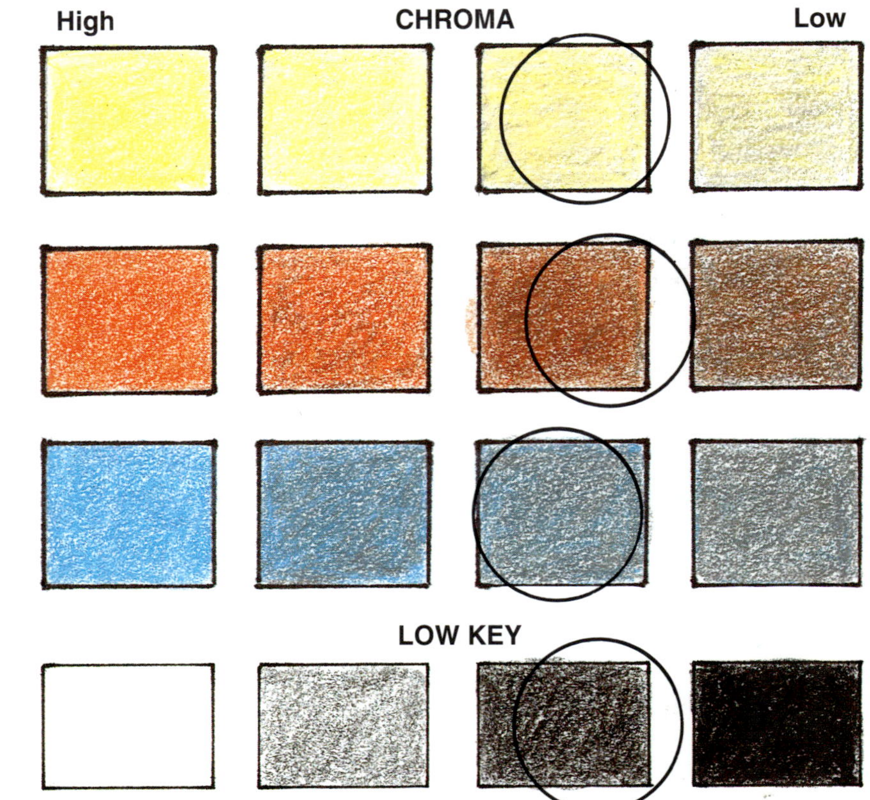

Notice the choice of colors for Bron and Anela. With Bron, bright colors are used to keep consistent with the high-key mood, while the lower keyed choice of colors for Anela is limited to burnt sienna, black, blue, grays, and a touch of red.

WARM/COOL CONTRAST

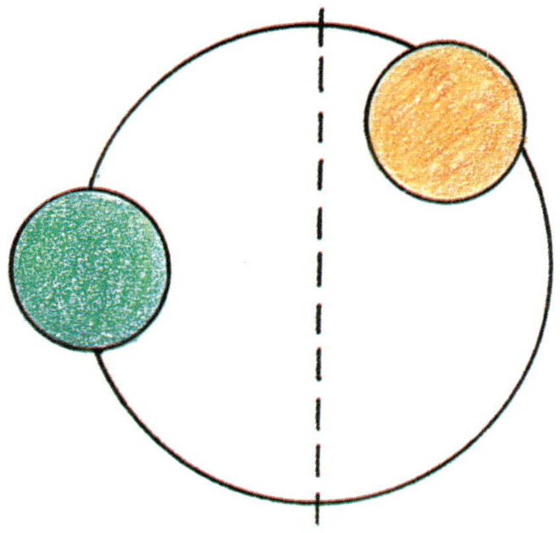

In nature we are surrounded by the effects of warm and cool contrasts: sunlight is yellowish, skylight is blue; heat expands, cold contracts; warm colors advance, cool colors recede. In painting, when we are trying to create an illusion of space, these principles are especially important.

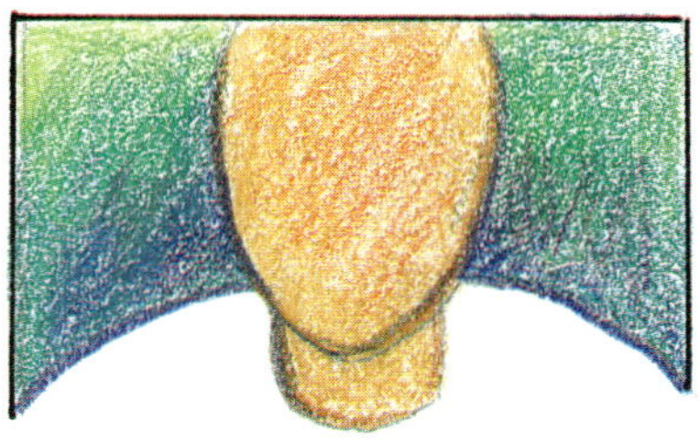

This simplified diagram shows how Paul's head advances as a warm shape against a cool background.

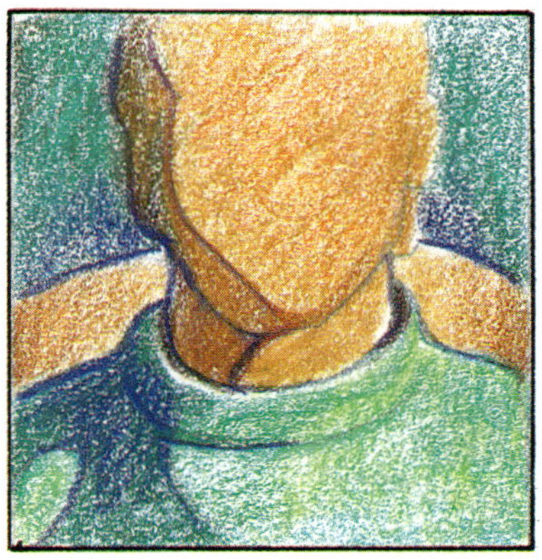

Here is an important principle known as "overlapping." The cool shirt overlaps the warm chair which overlaps the blue background, creating foreground, middle ground, and background space.

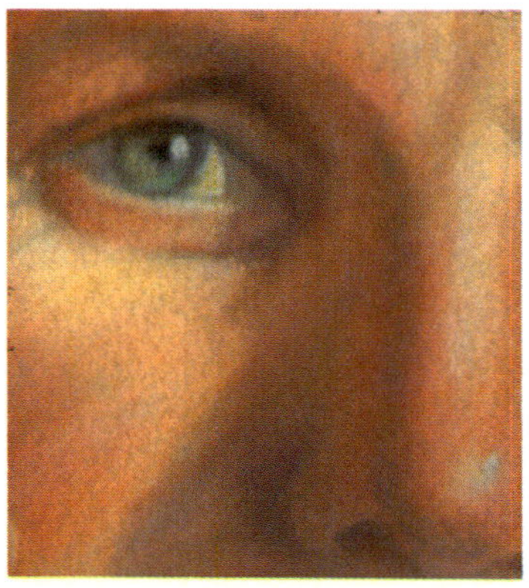

Even in the eye, warm and cool mingle: blue-green iris, highlight, pupil, and a yellowish reflected glow. Notice how the cool gray cast shadow reveals the three-dimensional shape of the eye.

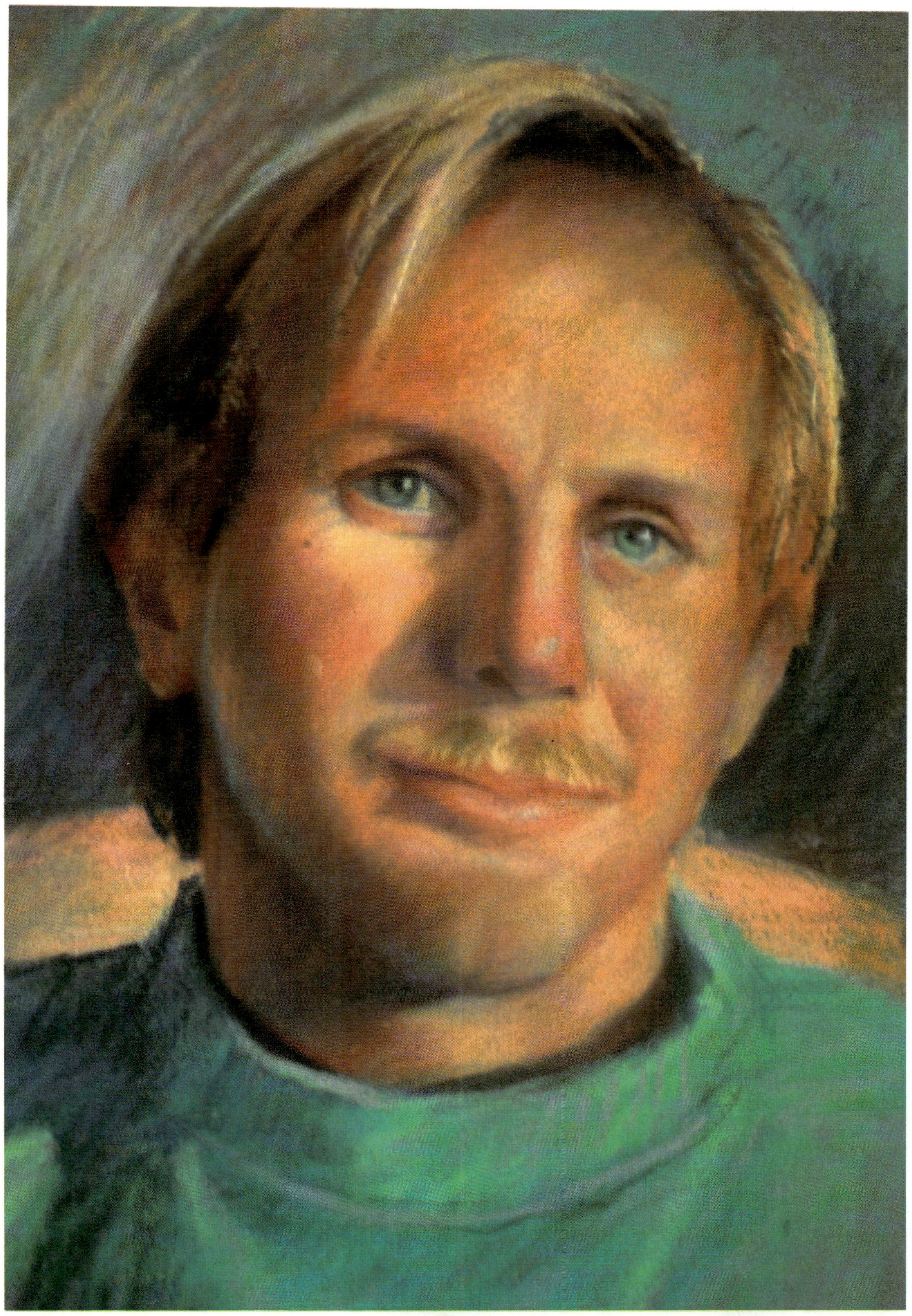

Paul Pastel On Paper 13 x 10

The examples of Paul and his son Bron (previous page) are both preliminary studies for a family portrait (Paul's wife and other son are not shown). Preliminary studies are helpful in getting to know the sitter and to work out problems of proportion, color, and composition. This degree of finish is accomplished by a combination of some rubbing and hatching and a lot of observation. Studies are usually fairly detailed when you are trying to gain an understanding of the underlying anatomy. Notice how the head shifts in hue from yellowish on the forehead to pinkish on the cheeks, nose, and ears, to grayish on the jaw. Most portraits of Caucasian men under warm light follow this formula because the yellow light is strongest up high, there is more circulation at the mid-area, and the chin has a "five o'clock shadow" and reflected light from the shirt.

PORTRAITS IN PROCESS...

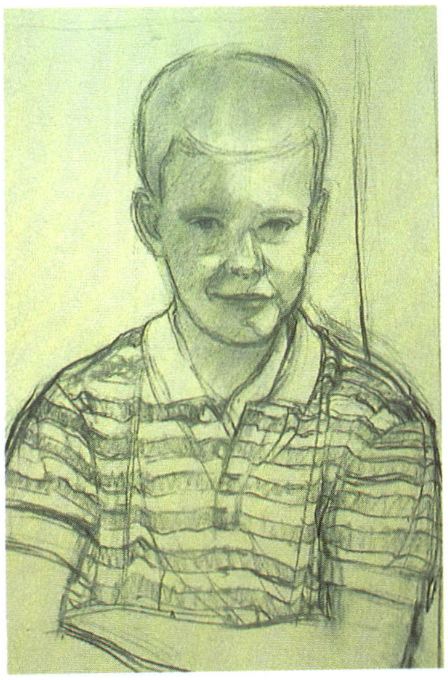

Using a sharpened vine charcoal stick, carefully sketch in every aspect of the portrait, including the stripes, collar, and shadow pattern. Vine charcoal is best for easily wiping away mistakes.

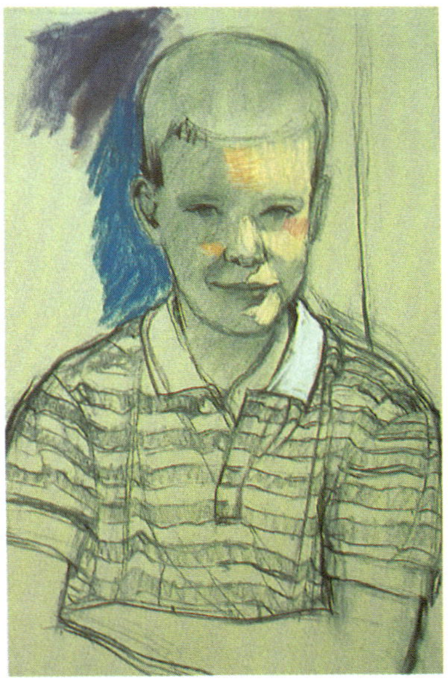

Use a dark brown pastel pencil to darken the eyelids, nostrils, lip line, and all other important dark points. Then put down the lightest light and darkest dark. All other values must fall between these extremes.

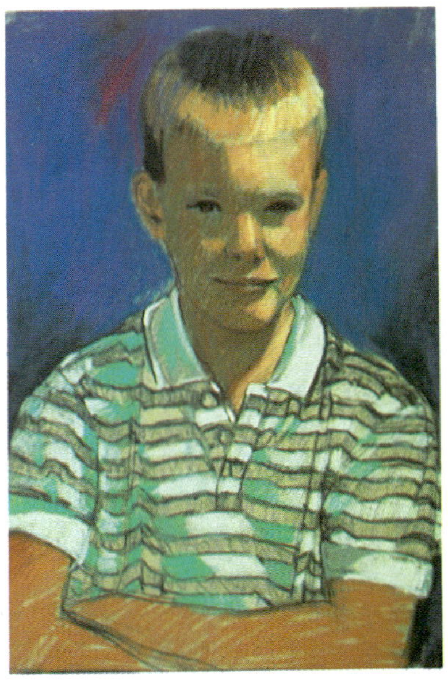

Mingle cool greens and burnt siennas into the flesh shadows: light burnt sienna for flesh lights, turquoise for the shadows of the white stripes, and vibrant colors in the background (they will be covered later).

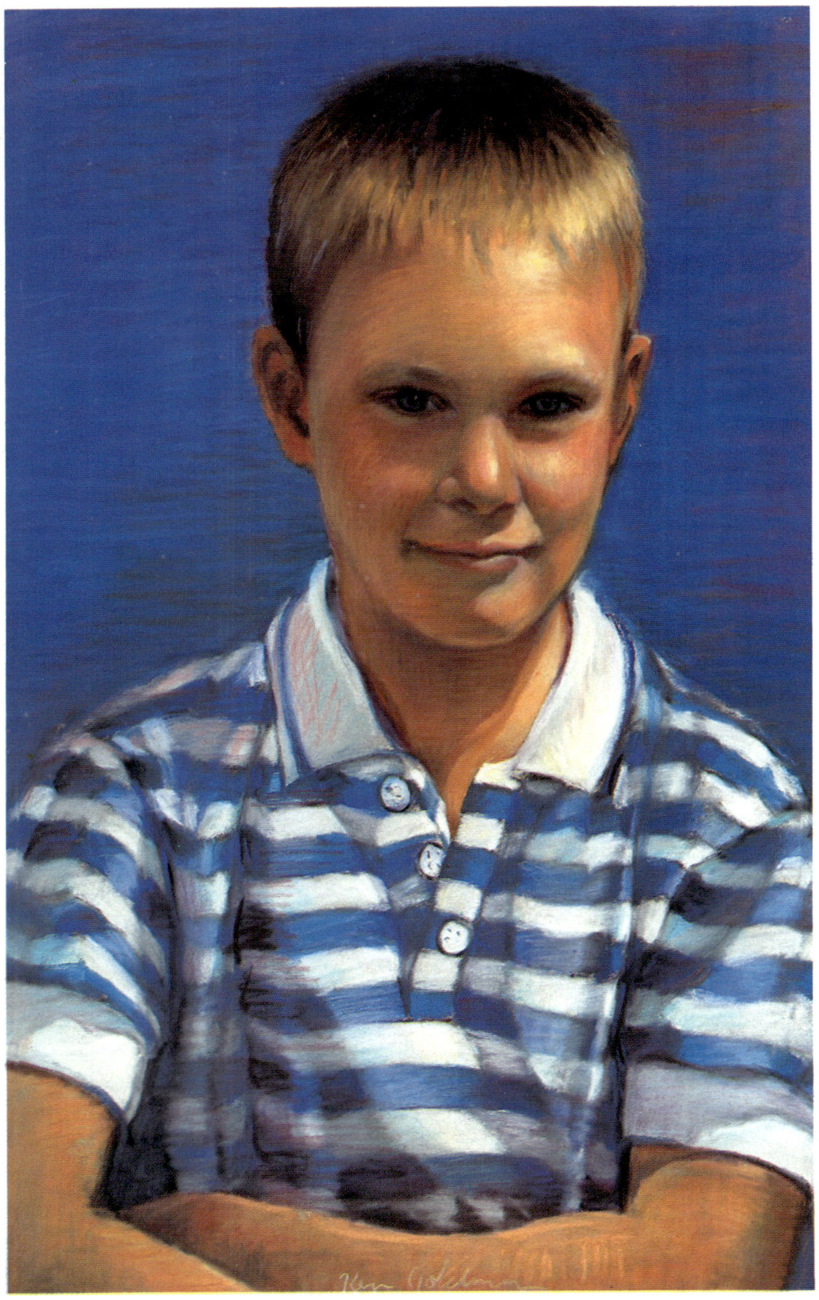

James Pastel On Dark Gray Pumice Board 16 x 10

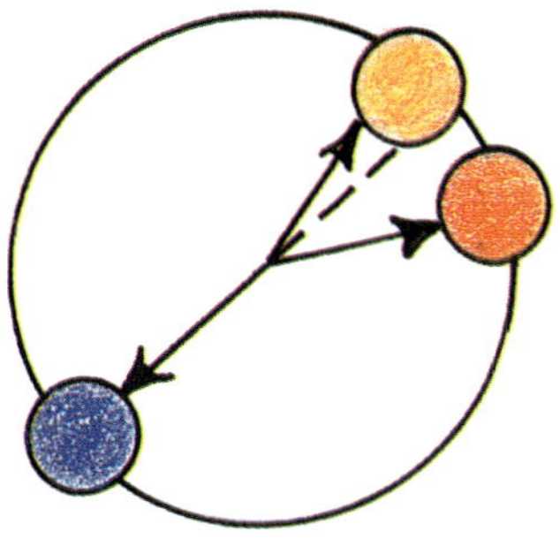

Like Brian's portrait on pages 11 and 17, this portrait is based on the complements of blue and orange, but it conveys an entirely different feeling. Notice how the burnt sienna (a dull orange complement of blue) that is feathered into the background softens the contrast.

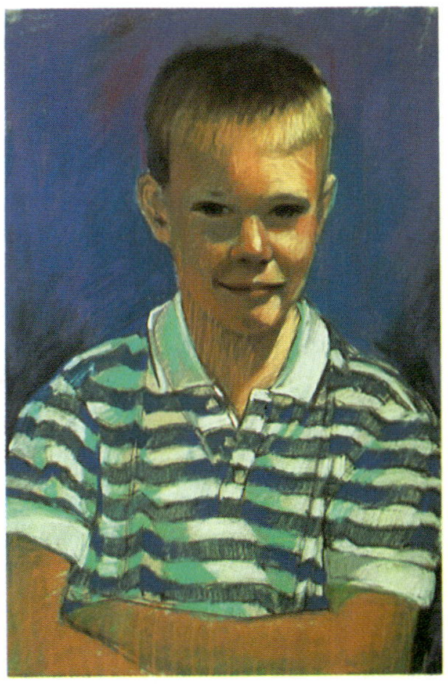

If necessary, reshape the head with the purple background color. Next, start adding the dark blue stripes, and then hatch back and forth with green, pink, and burnt sienna. Redefine the lids, nostrils, creases, and other accent areas.

For finishing touches, use a raw sienna pastel pencil to feather and blend the cheeks and forehead; some strokes follow the contours of form (see right side of face), while others are kept horizontal and vertical for design purposes (see neck, chin, and arms). The shirt folds are given dimension with form-following linear strokes of blue, gray, and pink. The flat blue background echoes the shirt and arms with horizontal strokes that also lead the viewer's eye to the head.

Perhaps you'll agree that James' face has a slight hint of mischief to it. With arms crossed, he kept sticking out his lower lip as a joke, and only toward the end of the session slipped into a decent expression which, in combination with his arm gesture, summed up his attitude about the experience.

The portraits of James, his sister, Theresa (page 15), and his brother, Brian (page 17), were commissioned to hang next to each other, so the color combinations were kept somewhat similar.

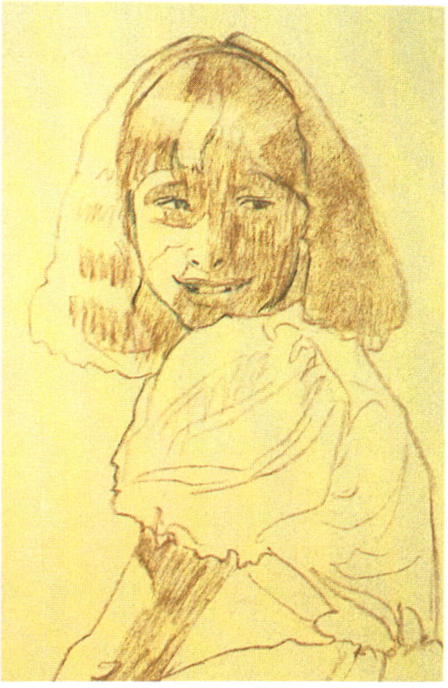

Sketch in lightly with vine charcoal, paying special attention to placement of the head over the body (drop imaginary vertical plumb lines to check alignments). Darken the shadow patterns and accent points, such as the lips and nostrils, etc.

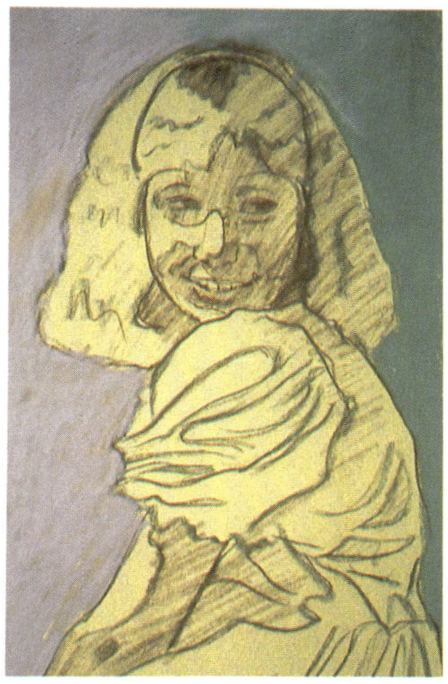

This drawing is actually a first attempt that ended up in the trash. However, it does demonstrate how to start a lay-in by first putting in the background color (it ended up much darker) and then relating other colors to it.

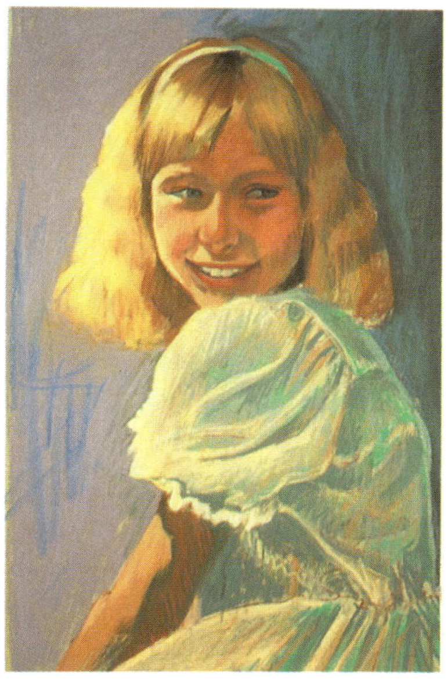

The edge of the sleeve is lightest; the hair is second; the face, arms, and dress shadows are middle values. Pink, turquoise, and raw sienna are good colors for the shadows of the luminous white fabric. The face is too red at this point.

This portrait was intended originally to be a lighter complementary contrast between yellow and violet. However, as the work progressed, darker violet seemed to bring out more luminosity and harmonized better with the other two portraits.

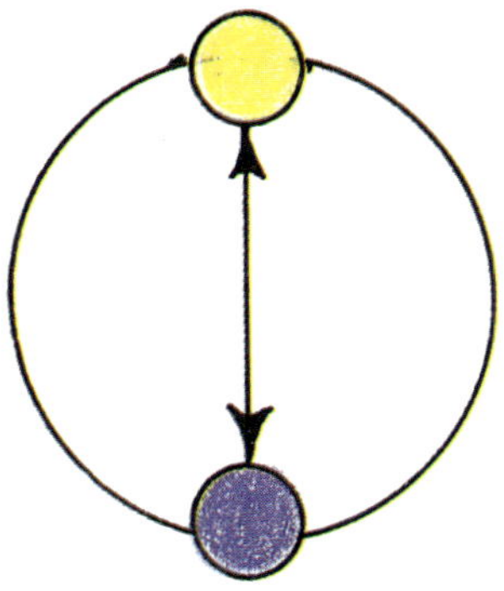

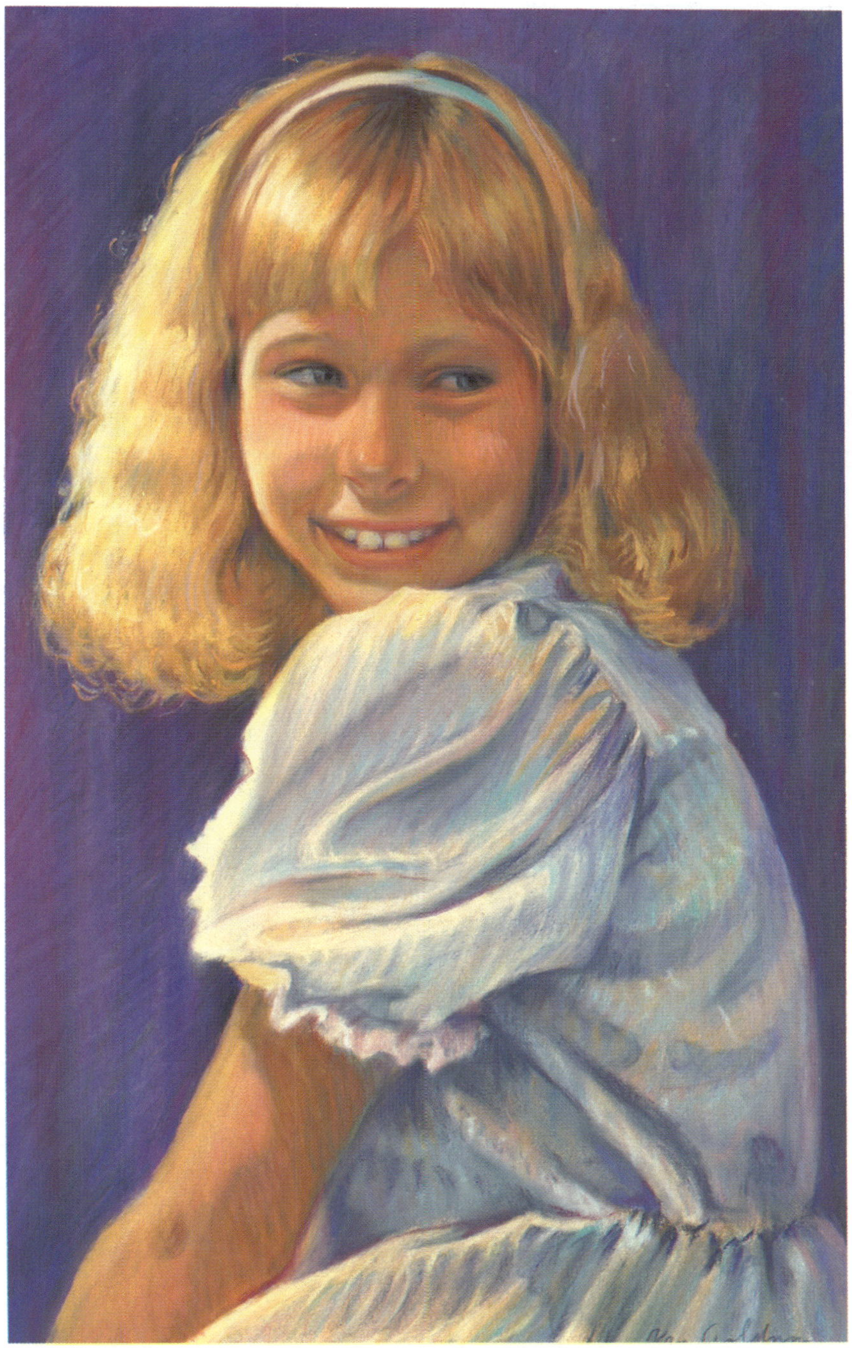

Theresa Pastel On Dark Gray Pumice Board 16 x 10

Finally, tone down the red face by feathering with green, gray, and ochre yellow pastel pencils. Bring out more light by darkening the background, and then add some light yellow and orange to the light rim of the dress (warms seem brighter than cools), and scumble purples over the blue to create a violet contrast to the glowing blond hair.

Theresa loves to pose. She hasn't a hint of shyness and in that way is every portrait painter's dream. However, having such a big natural smile can pose problems since it can look artificial and posed, but after a few minutes it was obvious that there was no other option except to let her fully express her delight. A young child's smile, especially at this awkward age, must be done carefully; too much detailed attention to new teeth can detract. You should treat the general mass of teeth like a semi-circular form that gets darker and grayer on the sides as it goes under the corners of the lips and make it lightest in the middle. Indicate the placement of every tooth, and then softly blend them together.

Setting a pose like this (where the model looks over her shoulder) is easy with photography, but would be difficult to hold in a sustained live sitting.

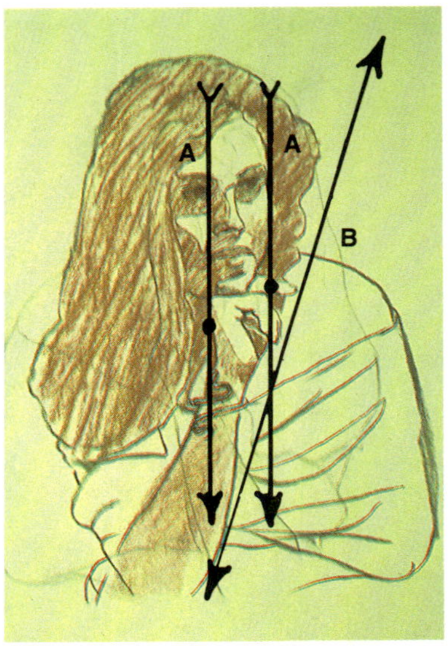

After lightly sketching with vine charcoal, check the placement and size of the hand by dropping imaginary plumb lines (A) and looking for continuing diagonals, i.e., line of arm and hair (B). Mass in darks and shadows with a brown hard pastel.

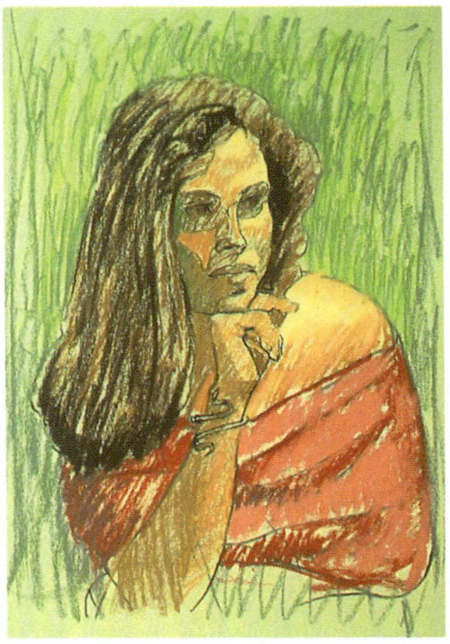

Using the tips of your hard pastels, block in five major areas: background, hair, blouse, light flesh, and shadow flesh. Knowing that the shadows will contain reflected red from the blouse, mass them in with red's complement—green.

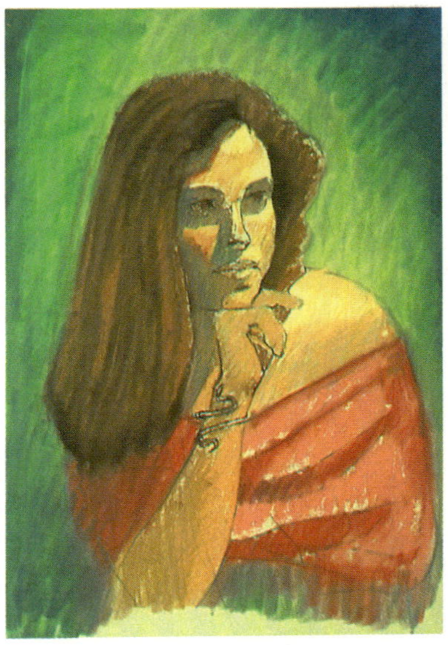

Continue to heighten the background with darker values and richer color relationships. Blend some areas with your finger or a chamois. Experiment with graying the shadows and placing strong reds at their edges.

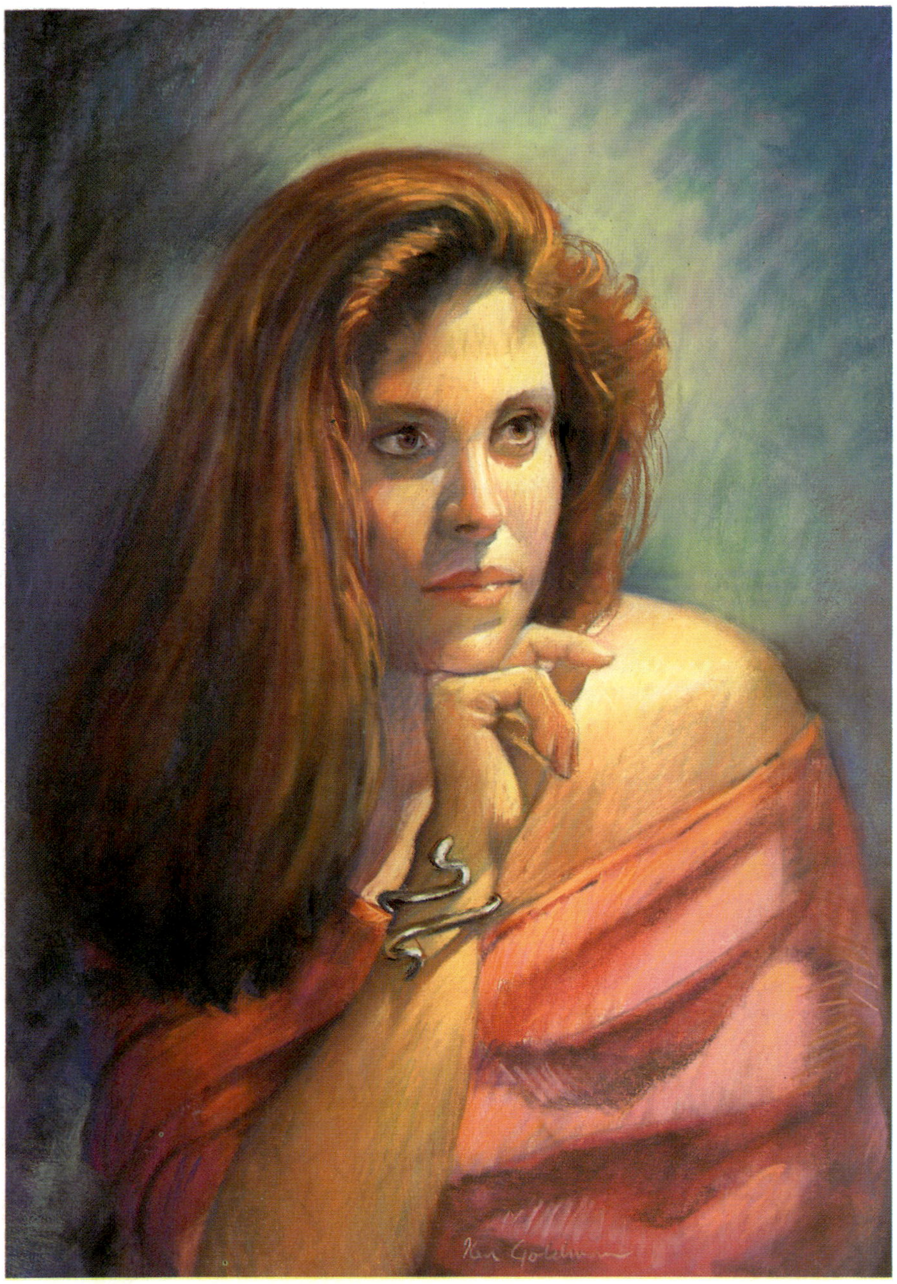

Elisa Pastel On Tan Pumice Board 20 x 14

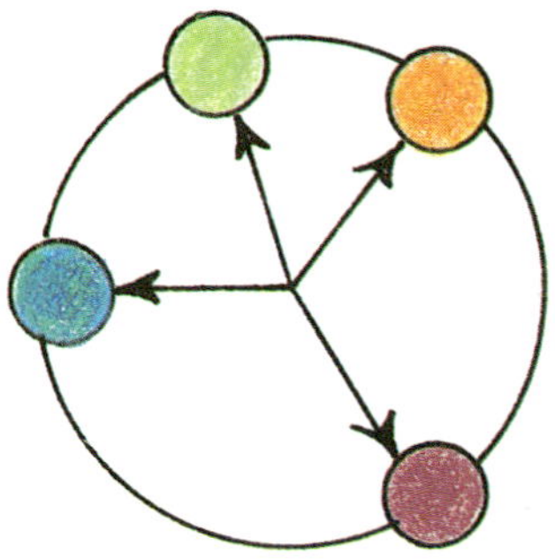

A mutual complementary color scheme has one dominant color complemented by three opposites.

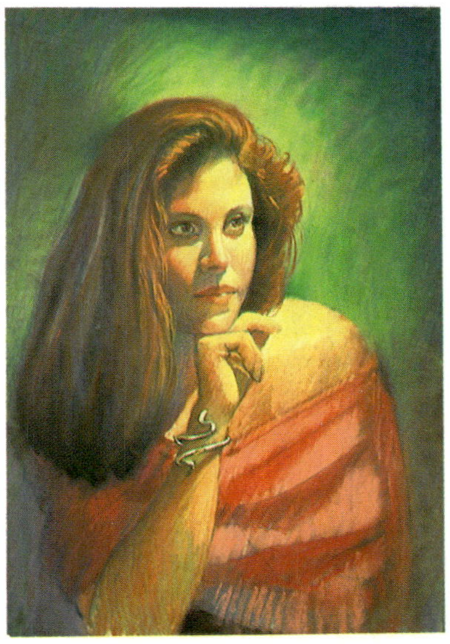

Begin to detail the eyes, nose, and mouth with pastel pencils; put green and red into the shadows. Intensify the lights and darks of the hair by adding orange and ultramarine blue. Gently scumble pink over the green background to enliven it.

During the final stage it is important to consider lost and found (soft and hard) edges. The right side of the hair and sleeve seem too isolated and are blended into the background. On the blouse, cast shadows are reshaped, shadow cores are darkened, reflected light is added to the left side, and form-following strokes are added to the folds. The index finger and palm were too indefinite, so they were reshaped with gray and red pastel pencils.

Elisa's mother is fond of the *chiaroscuro* (light and dark) lighting effects of Carravagio and Rembrandt. When she commissioned this portrait, she had these effects in mind, but she also wanted it very colorful. She was given a series of 3" thumbnail studies, each with varying color effects, and asked to choose one. Communication is extremely important; there's nothing worse than finding out, once the portrait is complete, that your choice of colors was great for you but not for the client.

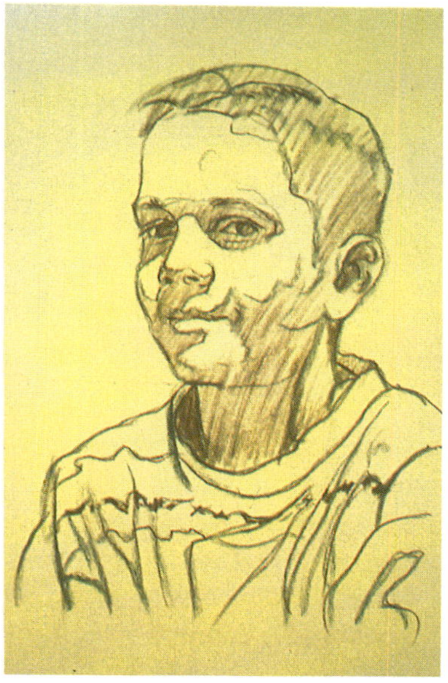

The initial drawing process here is basically like the three preceding portraits. Massing in shadow patterns at an early stage always helps because it makes you look at negative shapes.

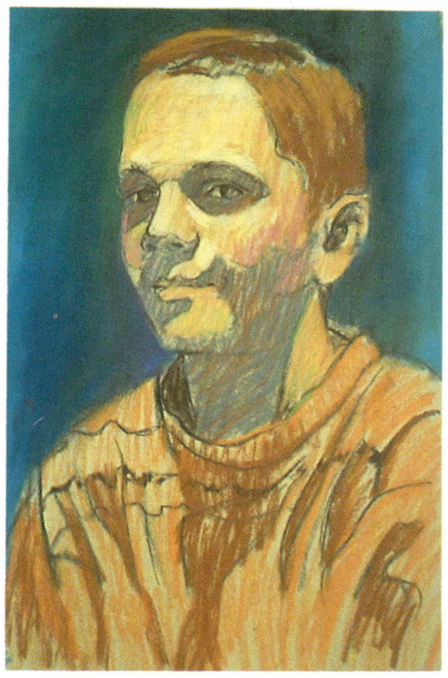

At this stage, begin to relate one color to another by adding the blue background, putting gray and red into the brown shadows, adding bright pink to the cheeks, and massing in the hair, light flesh, and shirt.

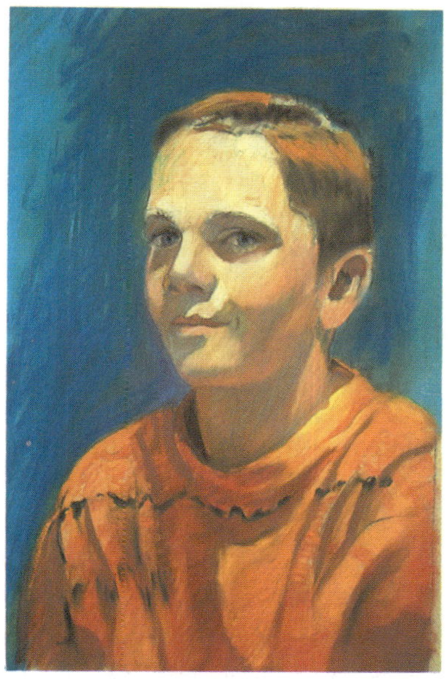

Now blend the shadows with a pastel pencil and your finger. Darken the eyelids, pupils, and hair; then put in the dark shirt stripe, taking care to have it go *into* and *over* all the folds.

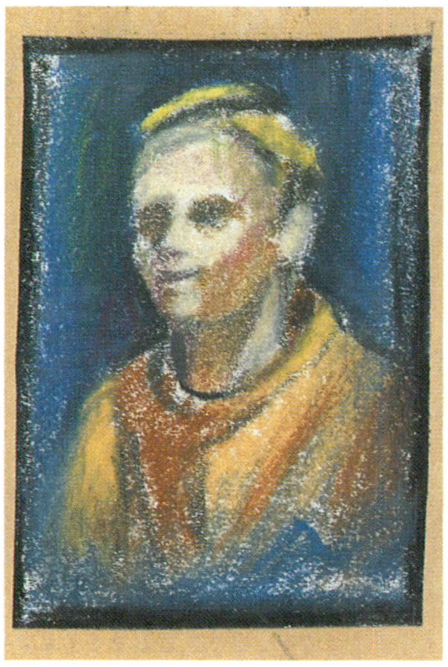

This is the preliminary value/color study sent to Brian's family for approval. Their only request was to lengthen the shirt to the base of the picture.

Any color can be used in a given area if the value is right. Brian's blond hair was accentuated with touches of purple and blue. The light head against the dark background made the picture seem flat; lightening the blue created atmosphere. Lightly scumbling purple over the blue background warmed the background a bit and helped relate it to the figure. Do you think this change added more depth?

Brian took his turn at modeling in stride. His enigmatic expression was about as far as his even-keeled enthusiasm allowed him to go, but he seemed to enjoy the experience. If you turn back the pages and compare all three portraits, the children's individual temperaments become apparent. With every new commission, even amongst family members, the mind must be emptied of pre-existing ideas about similarities. Each new portrait is a new challenge and it must be seen with fresh eyes; it is never easily solved with pat formulas.

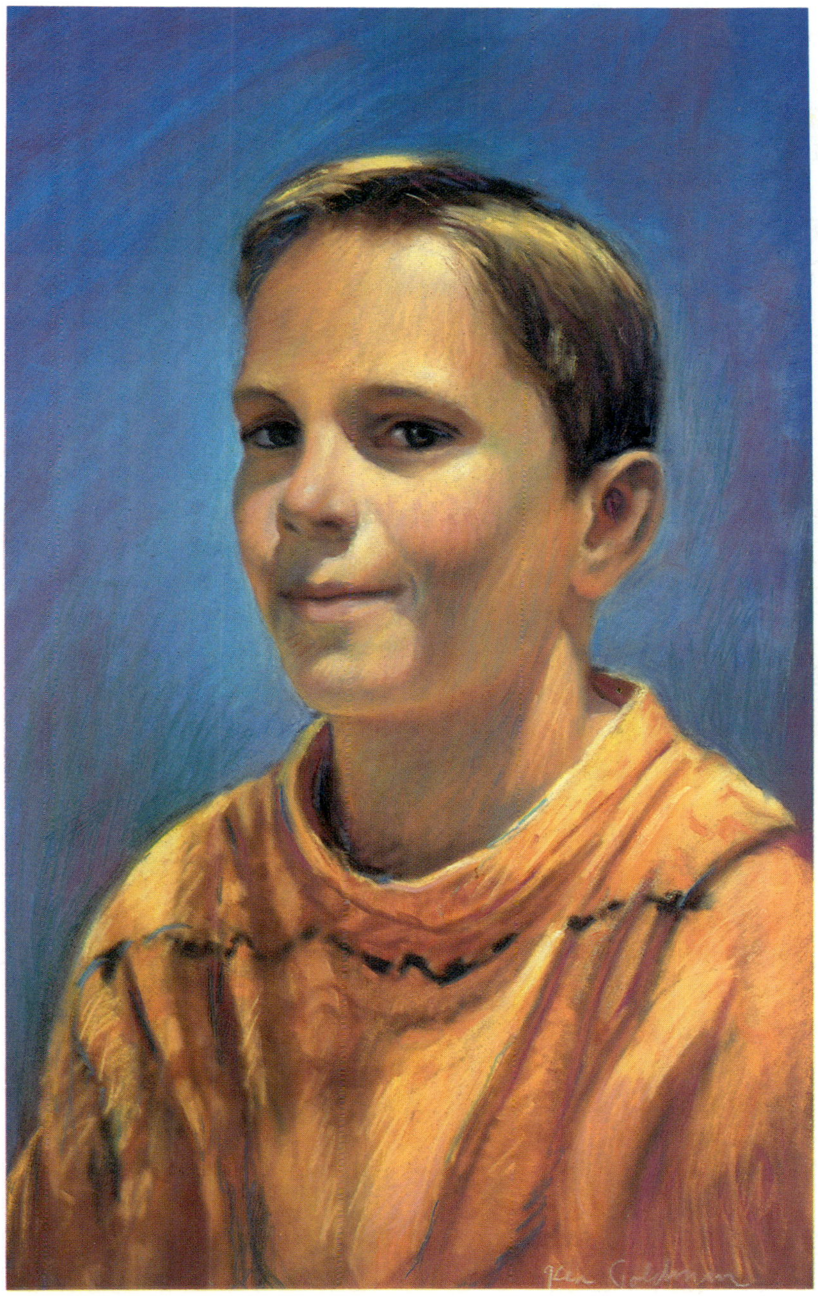

Brian Pastel On Dark Gray Pumice Board 16x 10

PROPORTIONS AND FEATURES

Generalized Guidelines—Use these measurements to begin a portrait, but check for individual variations before you darken the lines.

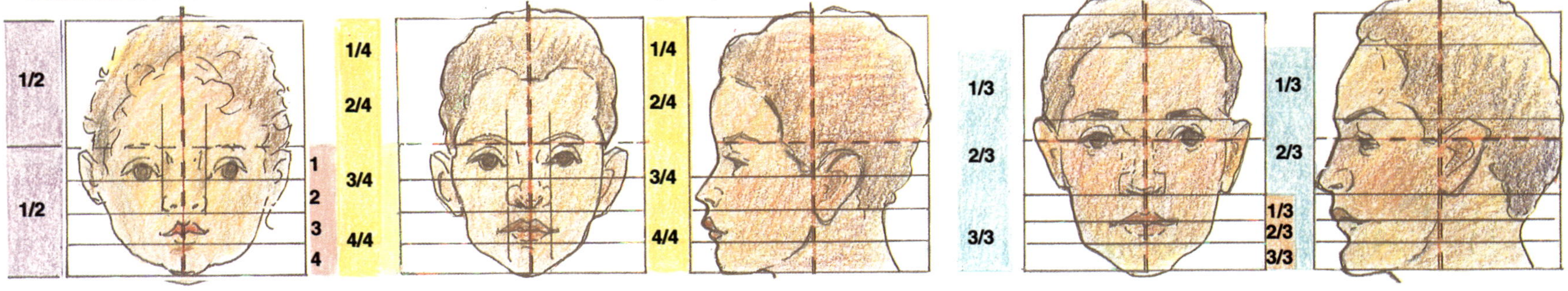

Baby—The jawbone, cheekbones, and nose are underdeveloped in relation to the cranium, so the whole face (brow to chin) fits below the midpoint of the head. However, the irises are fully-developed and they are spaced as far apart as an adult's.

Child—From the brow downward, a child's proportions are virtually the same as a baby's, except the longer face appears narrower, the ears are larger (they grow quickly), and the large eyes begin to look smaller.

Adult—On an adult, the lengthened face makes the eyes move up to the center of the head. For teens and adults, the measurement between the hairline and brow, the brow and nose base, and the nose base and chin base is equal (thirds).

STUDY THESE DRAWINGS: As The Head Direction Changes From A Front View To A Profile, The Nose Width Remains Constant (100%). Always Compare The Eye And Mouth Widths To The Nose; They Become Relatively Smaller As The Head Turns.

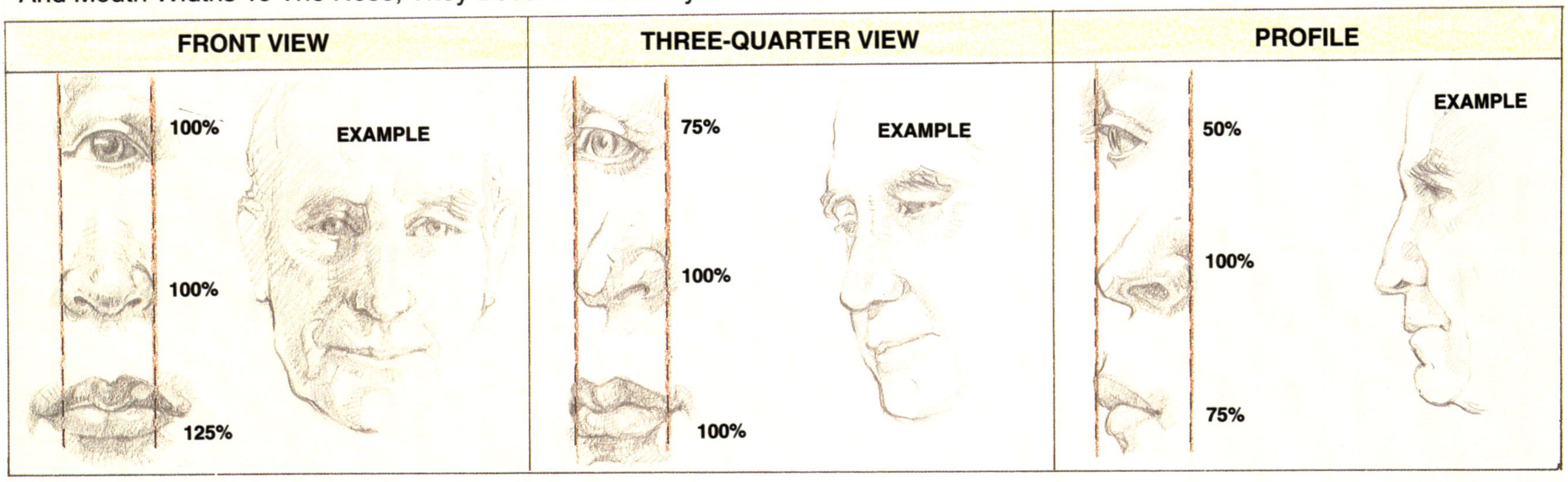

The superimposed ink lines on the five steps below show the thought processes during various stages of a portrait: (1) After finding the correct 1/3 divisions between hairline, brow, nose base, and mouth, draw a "T" and make sure that the brows, nose base, and mouth run parallel to its horizontal cross. (2) Look at the nose, mouth, eyes, etc., and search for basic forms (cubes, cylinders, spheres, etc.) that can be used as simplified representatives of the actual feature; for example, a combined cube and sphere is easier to draw than a nose. (3) Squint your eyes to see the overall simplified shadow pattern and mass it in. (4) Clean up and reshape the shadows with the outer contours of the lights. (5) Final pastel strokes should follow the contours of the forms in such a way that they reveal the underlying planes and muscles. Examine the portrait of George Washington on a dollar bill; the engraving lines are a perfect example of correct stroke directions.

1

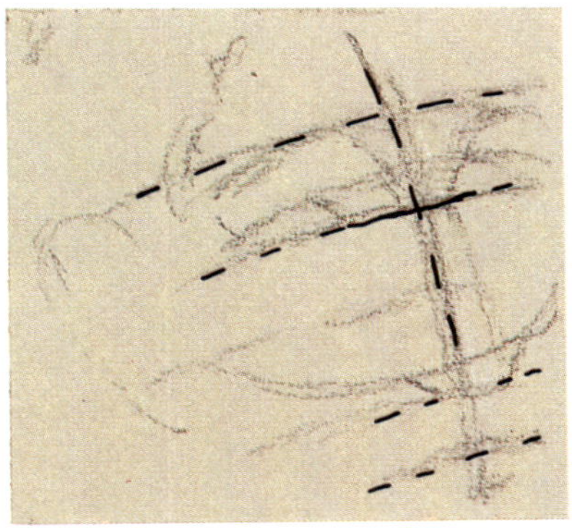

2

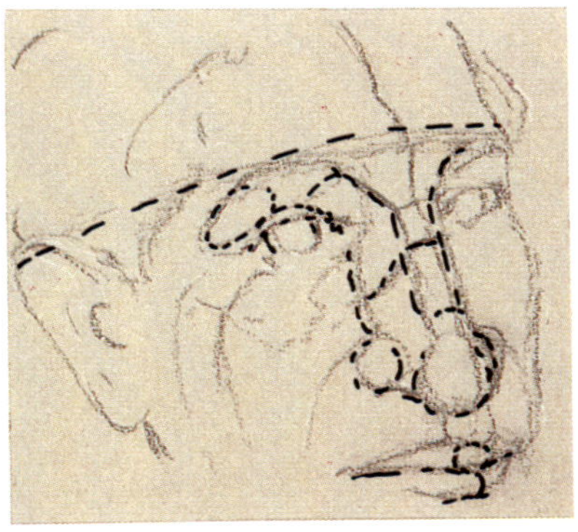

3

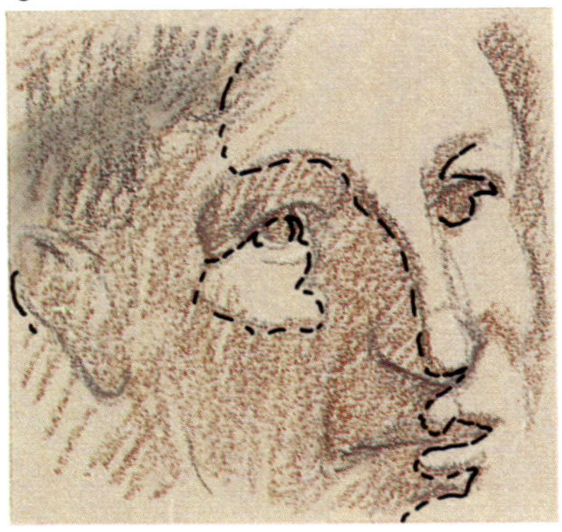

4

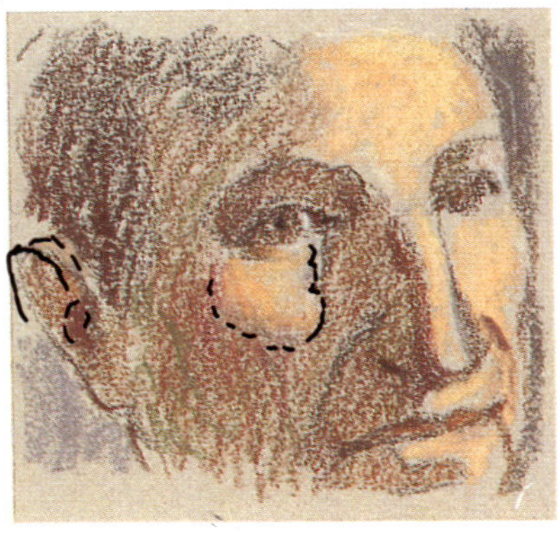

5

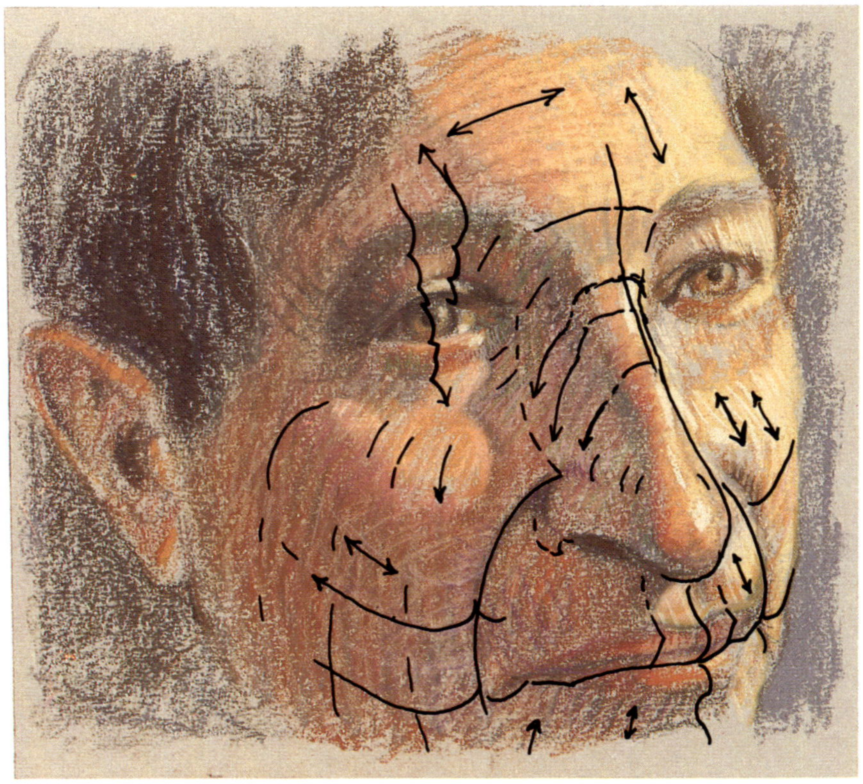

FEATURES AND THEIR ANATOMY

When studying the features, try to become familiar with their anatomy because underlying structure influences everything you see on the surface. Although this study is often considered dull, it can actually be quite exciting when you think about the body's incredible design. All visible forms of the body are affected by bone. Feel your own face for a moment. Anything hard is bone; anything semi-mobile is cartilage; the rest is muscle or tissue. Once you understand the logic behind muscular origins and insertions into or around certain bones, and then practice drawing them, your hand will become more deft, allowing you to draw the features with greater assurance and skill. This is why it is advisable to study artistic anatomy (see Walter Foster book #29, *Anatomy*).

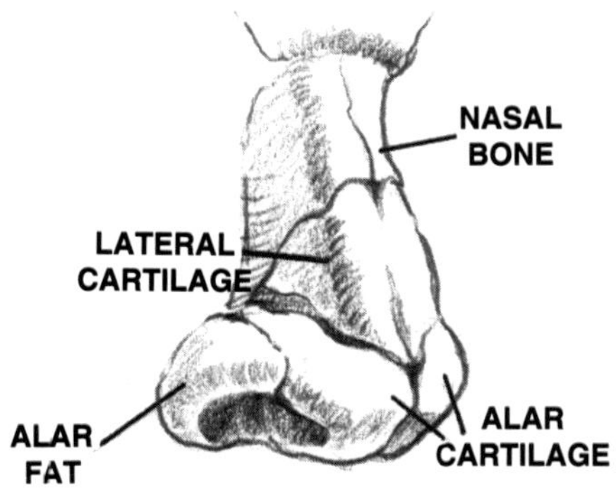

Feel your nose for differences between bone, cartilage, and fat. Then try drawing it.

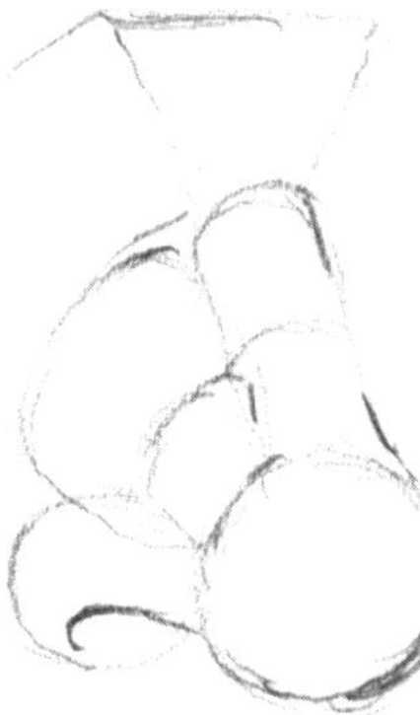

Translate what you see into cubes, spheres, and cylinders. Sketch lightly.

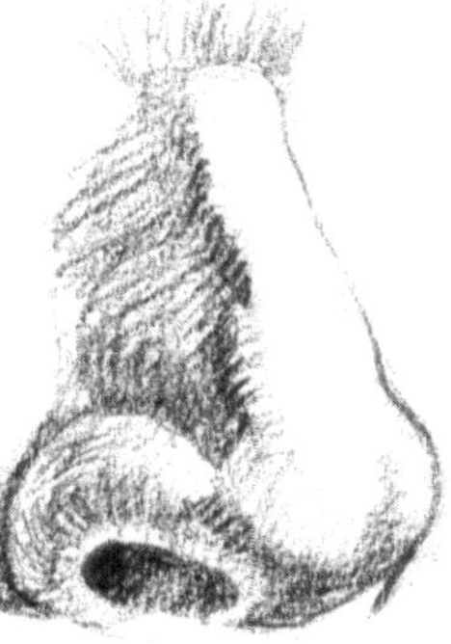

Add tone and accent the shadow core (the edge where light meets dark).

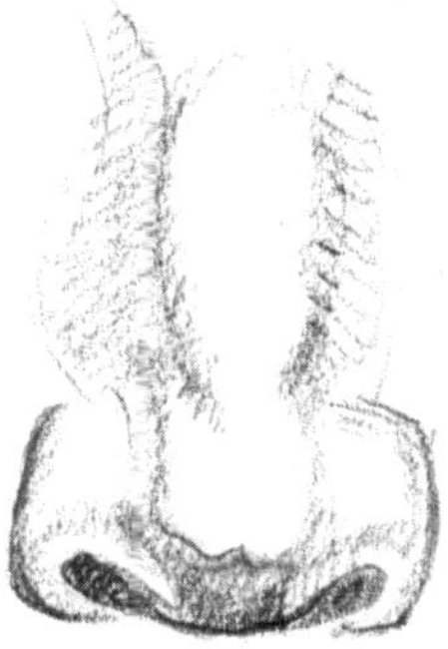

Study the front view in relation to the three-quarter view.

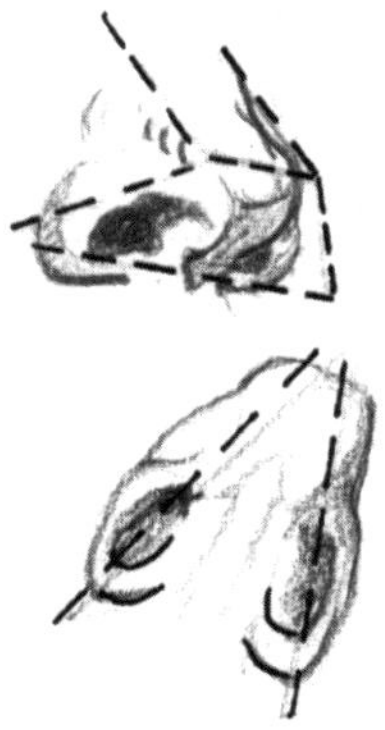

Use a hand mirror to observe how your nostrils look from below.

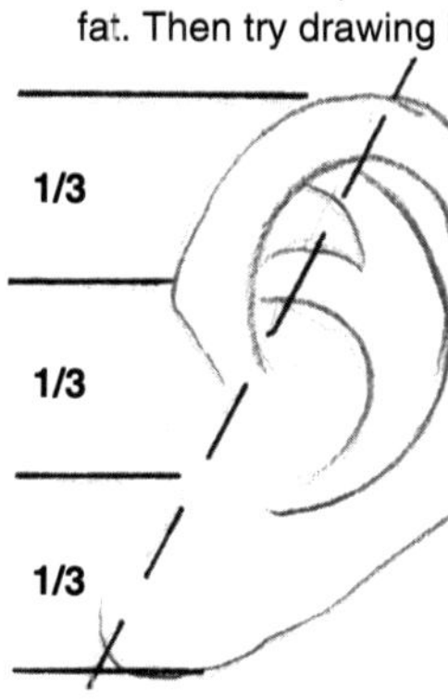

When drawing the ear, notice how it slants back and is divided into thirds.

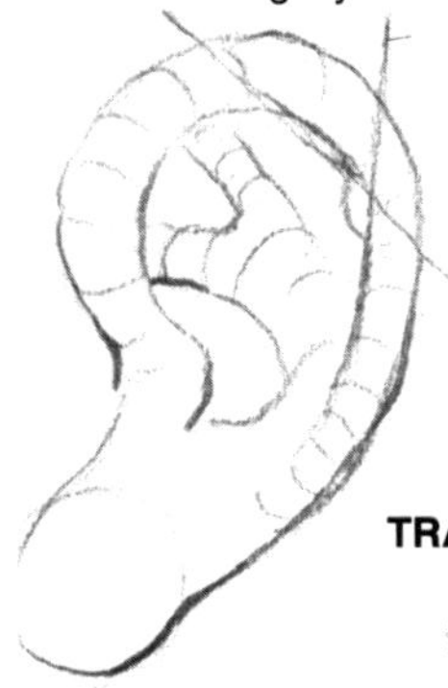

Ear forms are simply modified cylinders.

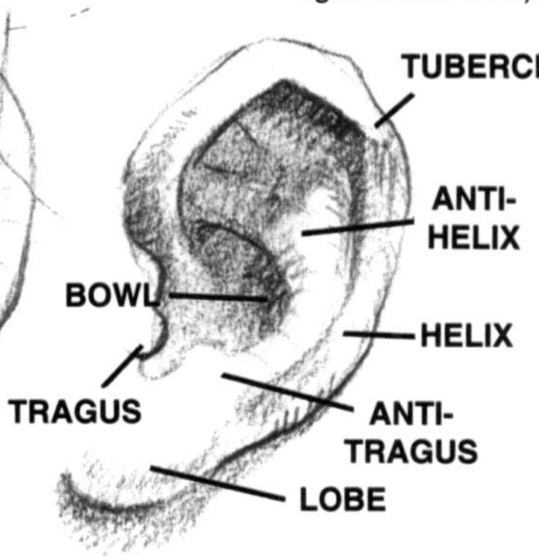

The ear and its parts.

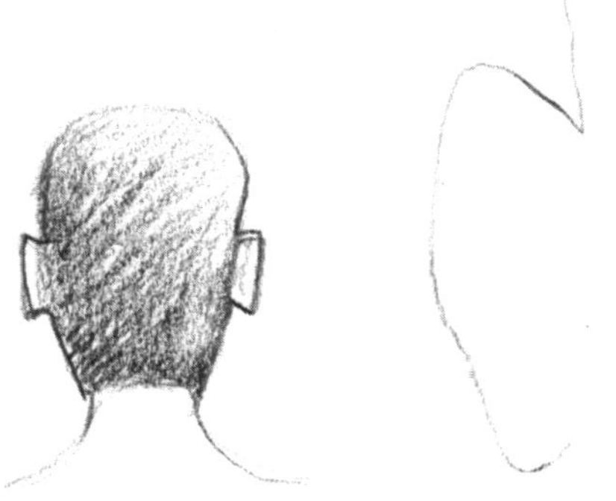

Ears are like discs.

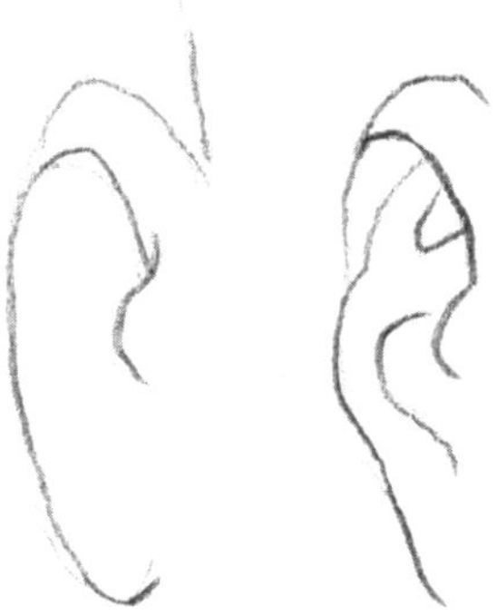

Sketch the silhouette; add the helix and tragus; then draw the anti-helix, bowl, and lobe.

Eyes and lips are grouped together because the eyelids operate quite similar to the lips. Eyes are muscle and skin pulled around a spherical eyeball, and lips are pulled around the semi-curved teeth. When you draw the features, follow these steps: (1) look long and hard at the feature; (2) find the correct angles and proportions, and then determine the simple form (cube, sphere, cylinder, etc.) and lightly sketch it; (3) redefine the contours of the simple form to more closely resemble the *actual* form; (4) add tone. Practice drawing features from all angles in many perspectives. Draw linear cross contours on eggs, balls, tissue rolls, and blocks. Then set up a side light and practice drawing them with outer and cross contours included.

EYEBALL

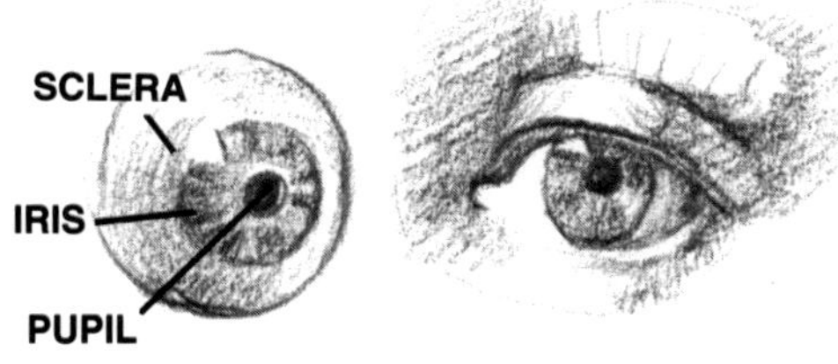

THREE-QUARTER VIEW EYEBALL

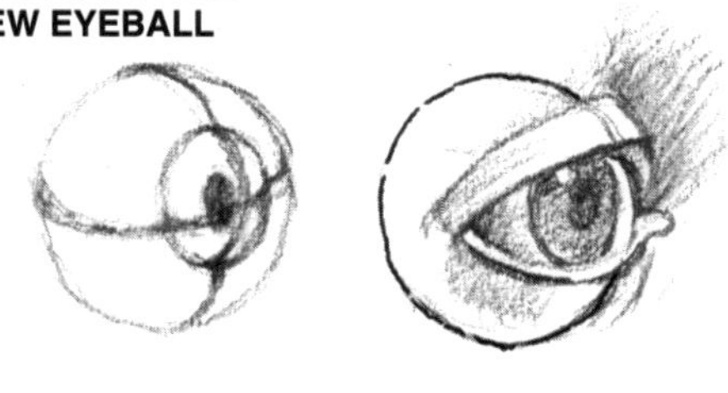

PROFILE SHOWING BULGE OF THE CORNEA

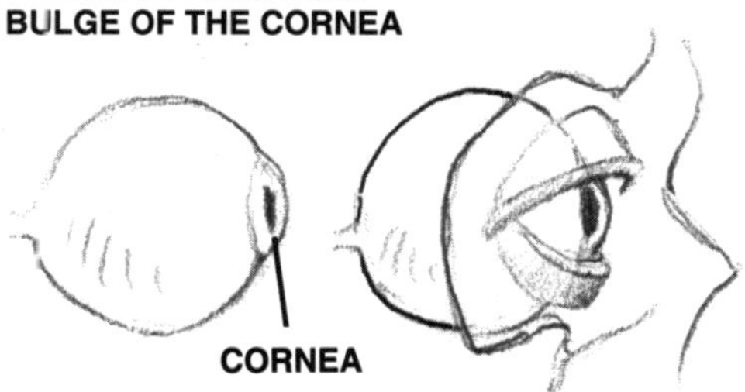

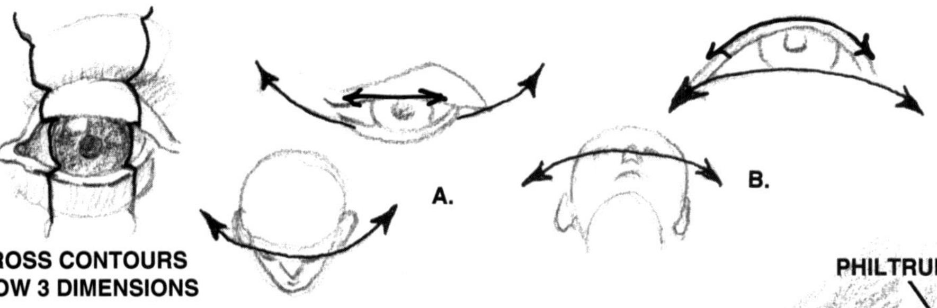

CROSS CONTOURS SHOW 3 DIMENSIONS

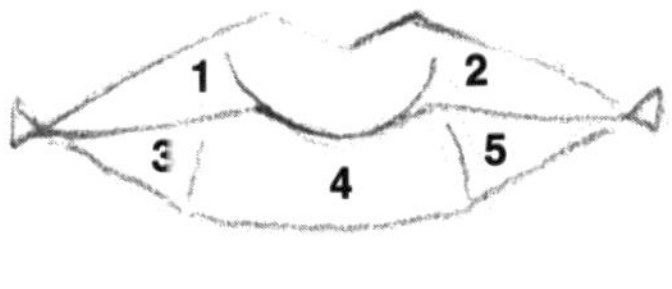

FRONT VIEW AND FIVE PLANES OF THE LIPS

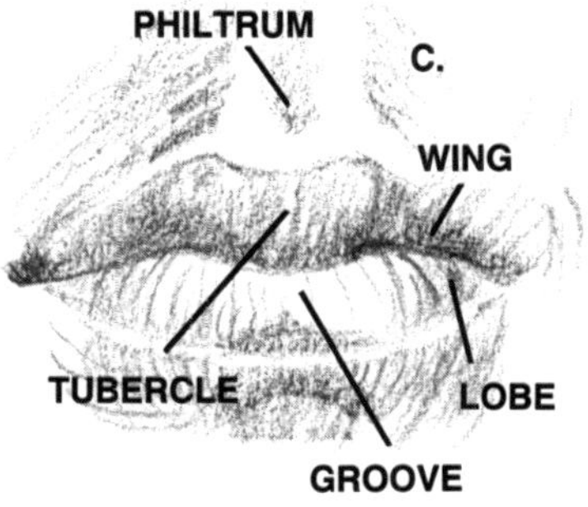

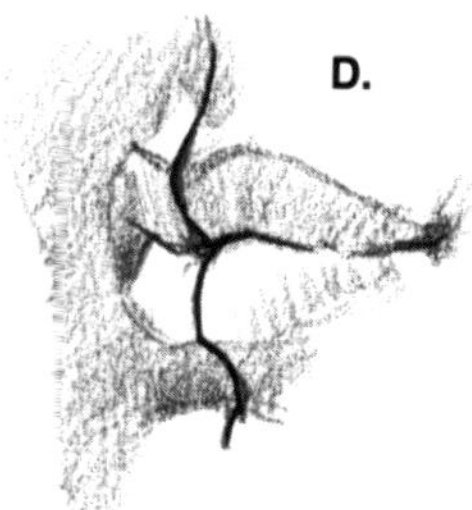

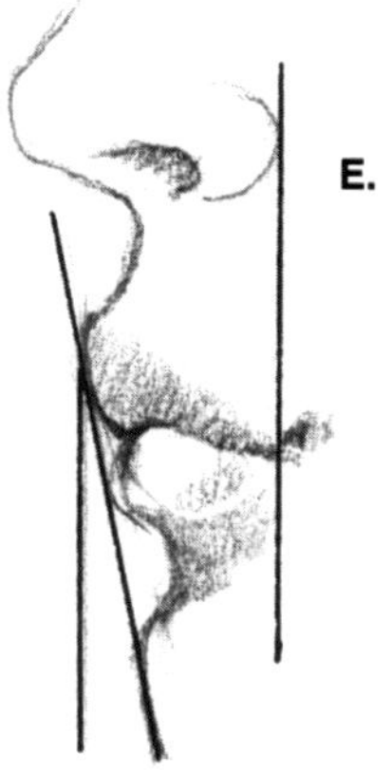

When the head looks down, the ears rise above the brow line and the bottom eyelid is more curved than the upper eyelid (A). When the head is seen from below, it is just the opposite (B). Here are some anatomical parts of the mouth (C), and a three-quarter view (D); notice how the upper tubercle fits into the lower groove. The upper lip usually protrudes more than the lower lip, like the teeth (E). The chin is usually behind the lips, and the corner of the mouth sits behind the nose.

WORKING IN COLOR FROM BLACK-AND-WHITE

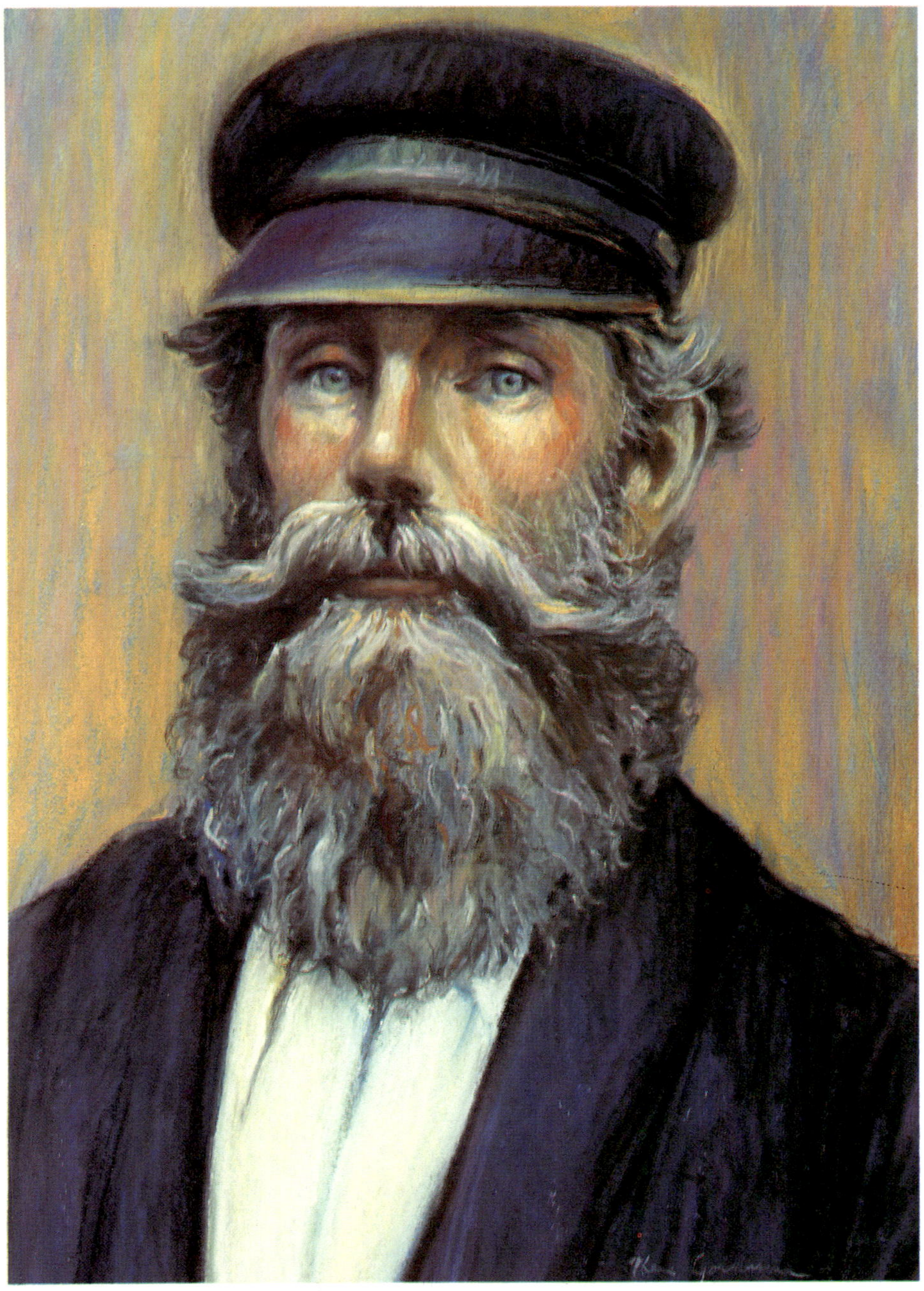

Captain Wm. Harrison Parrish Thompson Pastel On Paper 16 x 11

Translating this weathered photo of a Civil War captain into color was an interesting challenge. You may want to try this with your own black-and-white photo. If you look at this value scale, you will see that each tone can be assigned a definite color, which shows that black-and-white photos or tonal drawings make an excellent basis for color interpretations.

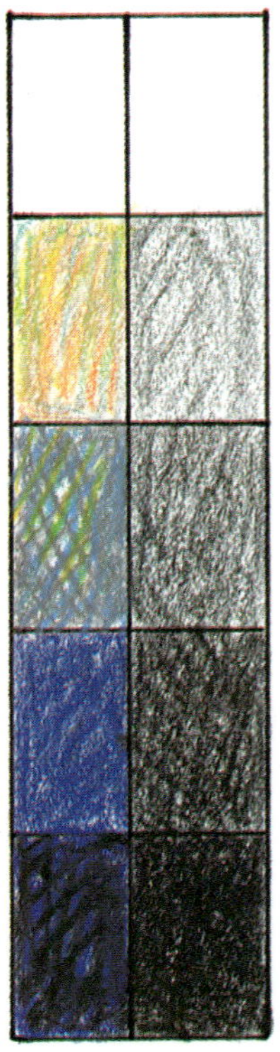

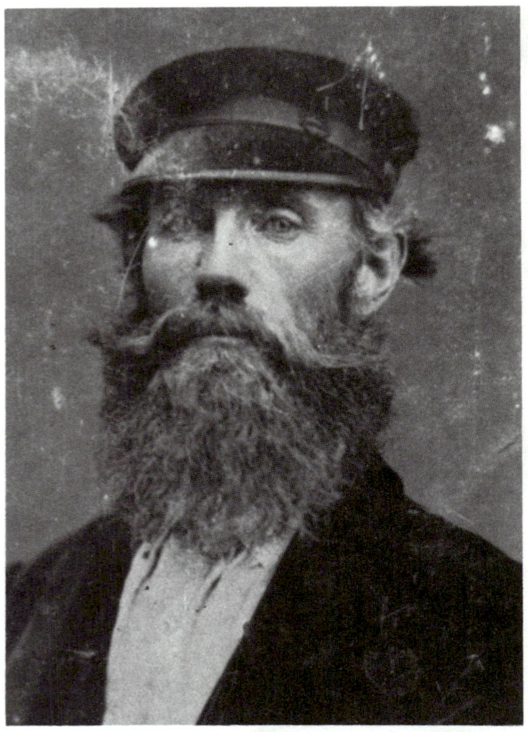

In this photo, the primary difficulties were to correctly show a slight turn of the face, to decipher and redefine the right eye, and, mostly, to attain the captain's look of pride. When you work from a photo, it is important to analyze each shape as if it were three-dimensional so you don't end up with a flat copy. Take the beard, for example. Most people are unaware that beards have distinct growth tracts and don't give its various layers serious thought. The tracts are analyzed and named below to show the importance of thinking in three dimensions.

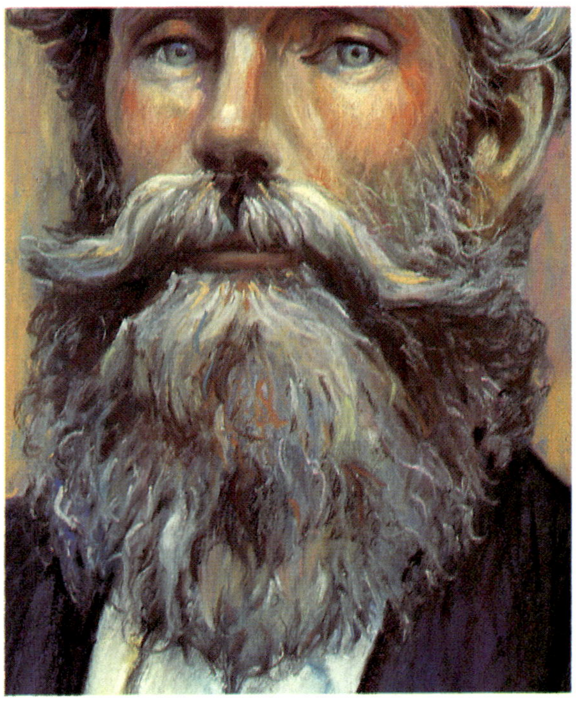

Notice the wide selection of colorful accents that are used to liven up the captain's gray beard. Compare the "dimensionality" of this "interpreted" beard to the black-and-white photo it came from.

THE SEVEN GROWTH TRACKS OF A BEARD

#1 **sideburns** merge with #2 **cheek hair**; #3 **moustache** overlaps #4 **corner of chin**; #5 **goatee** overlaps #6 **chin hair** (bushy area), which overlaps #7 **throat hair** and makes for beard length.

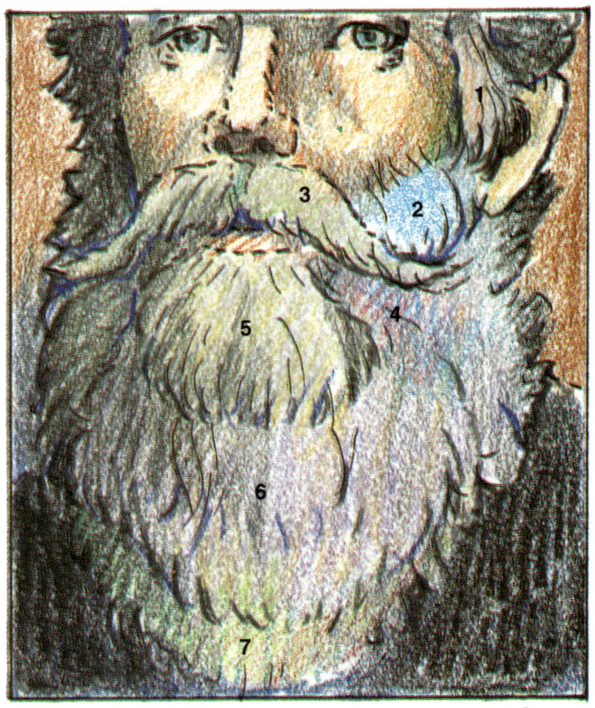

Each number on this drawing corresponds to one of the seven overlapping growth tracts.

FORM AND CAST SHADOWS

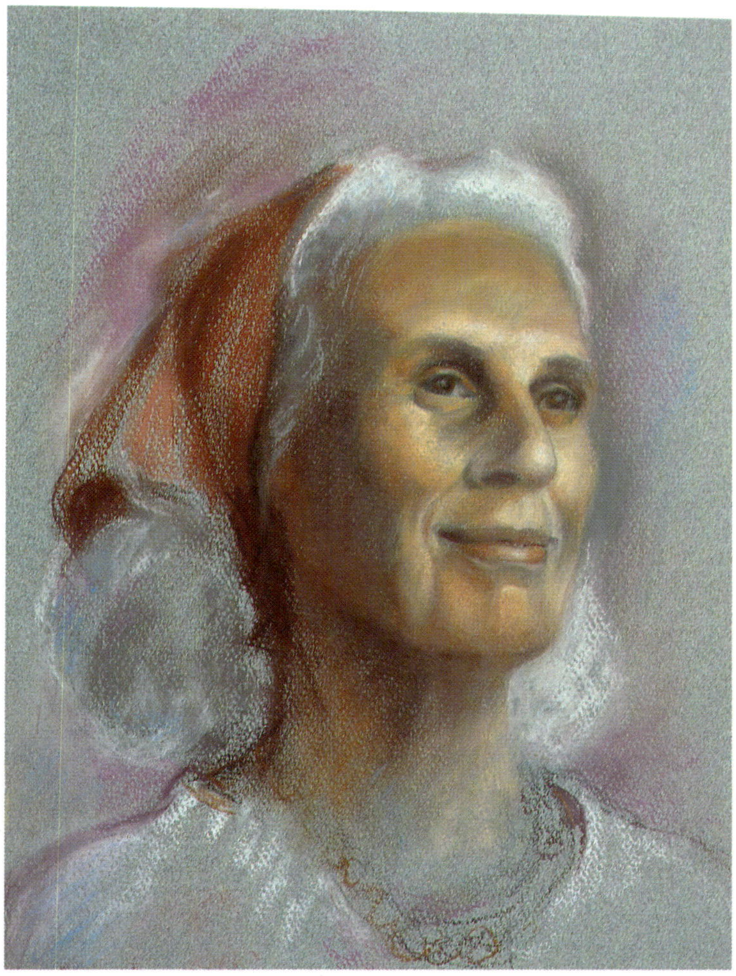

Maxine Goldman Pastel On Gray Paper 12 x 9

This portrait and the accompanying diagrams show how form shadows work in portraiture. As the front plane (A) turns into a side plane (B), the light gradually darkens. Its absolute transition is called the "shadow core" (C) and is an artist's greatest aid for showing volume.

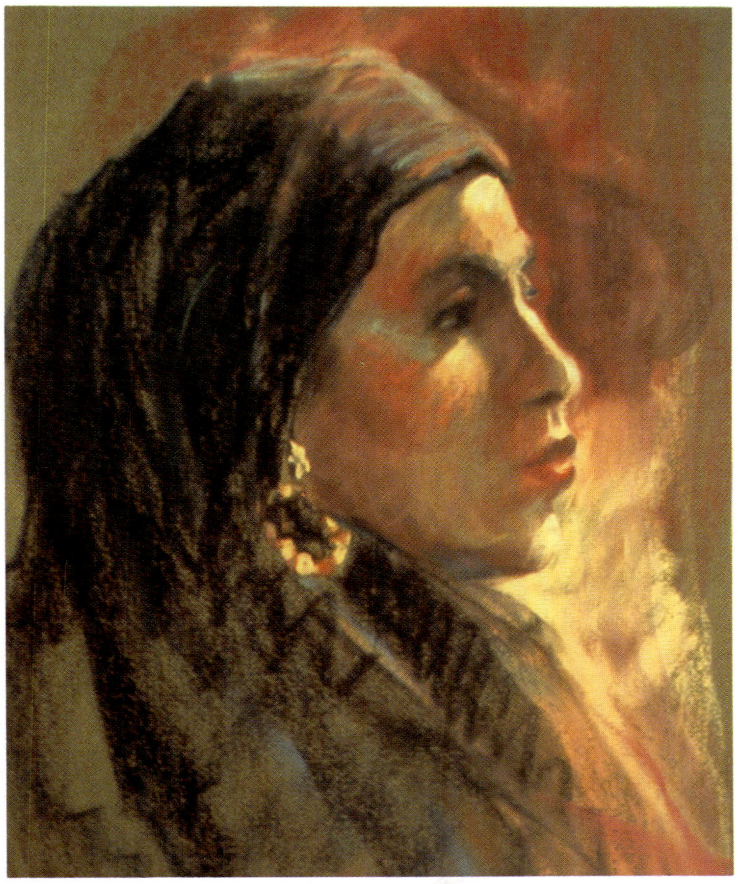

Study for a Gypsy Pastel On Green Paper 16 x 14

In this portrait, the scarf casts a shadow onto the forehead (1), the eyebrow casts shadow onto the cheek (2), and the lower lip throws a shadow onto the chin (3). Notice that these cast shadows are darkest at their point of origin and grow lighter and softer as they leave their source.

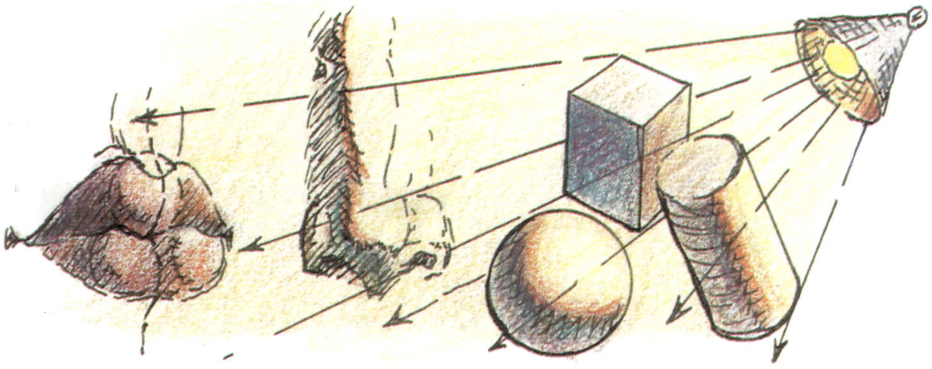

A **form shadow** occurs when objects or forms face away from the light (top diagram). Shadow shapes are determined by light direction and the physical shapes of various forms. Think of the effects of light and shadow on an egg; then relate them to the head below. Memorize the following rule about form shadows: "The lightest light in a shadow area (1) should always be darker than the darkest tone in the light area (2)." This means that the reddish reflected light in the shadow (1) must be darker than the darkest area of the light (2).

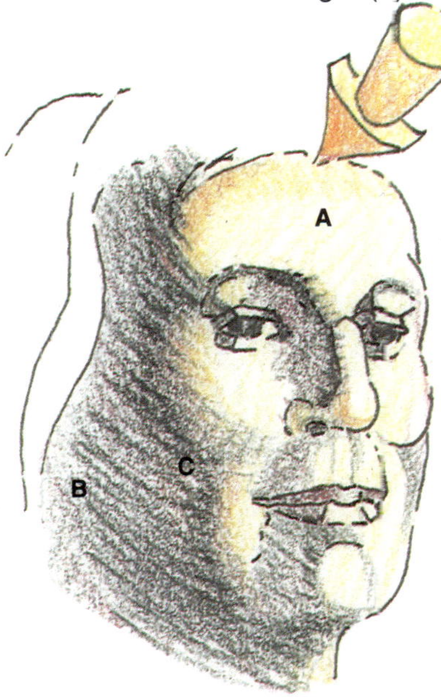

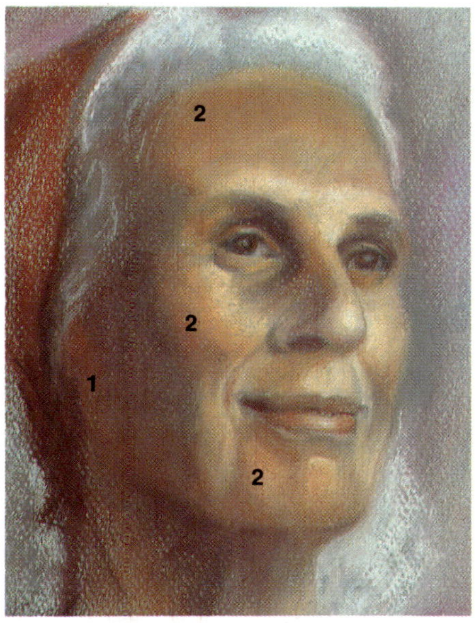

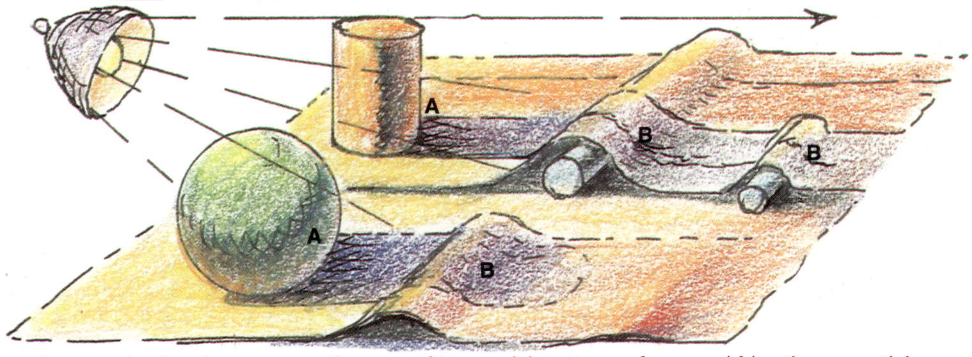

As cast shadows are thrown from objects or forms (A), they mold themselves perfectly to the surfaces they land on (B) and must be drawn carefully or they won't properly reveal these forms. A poorly-placed or overly dark cast shadow is much worse than no cast shadow at all and can easily ruin your portrait. If you see a cast shadow on your model but it doesn't seem useful in revealing form, eliminate it.

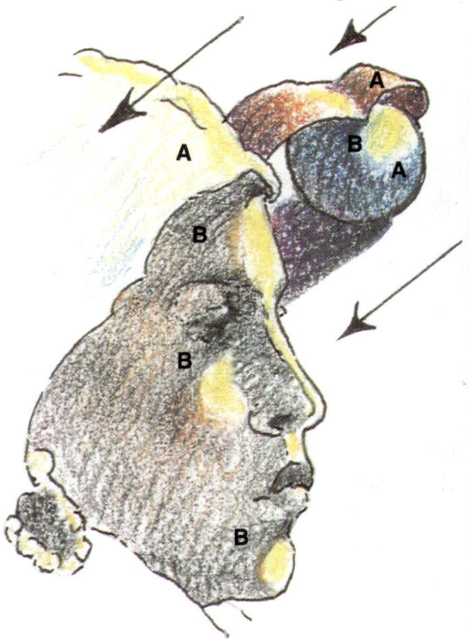

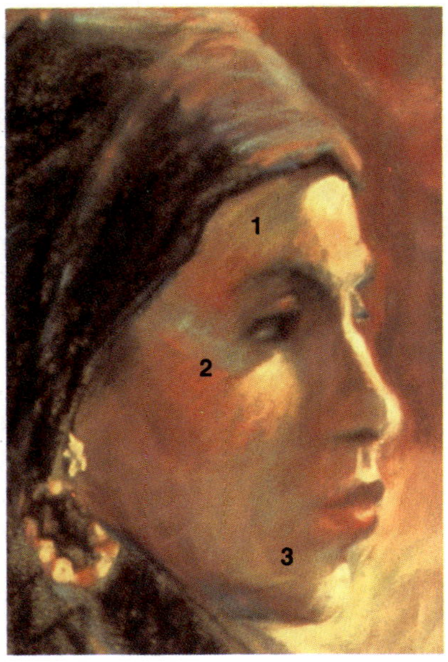

CREATING IMPACT

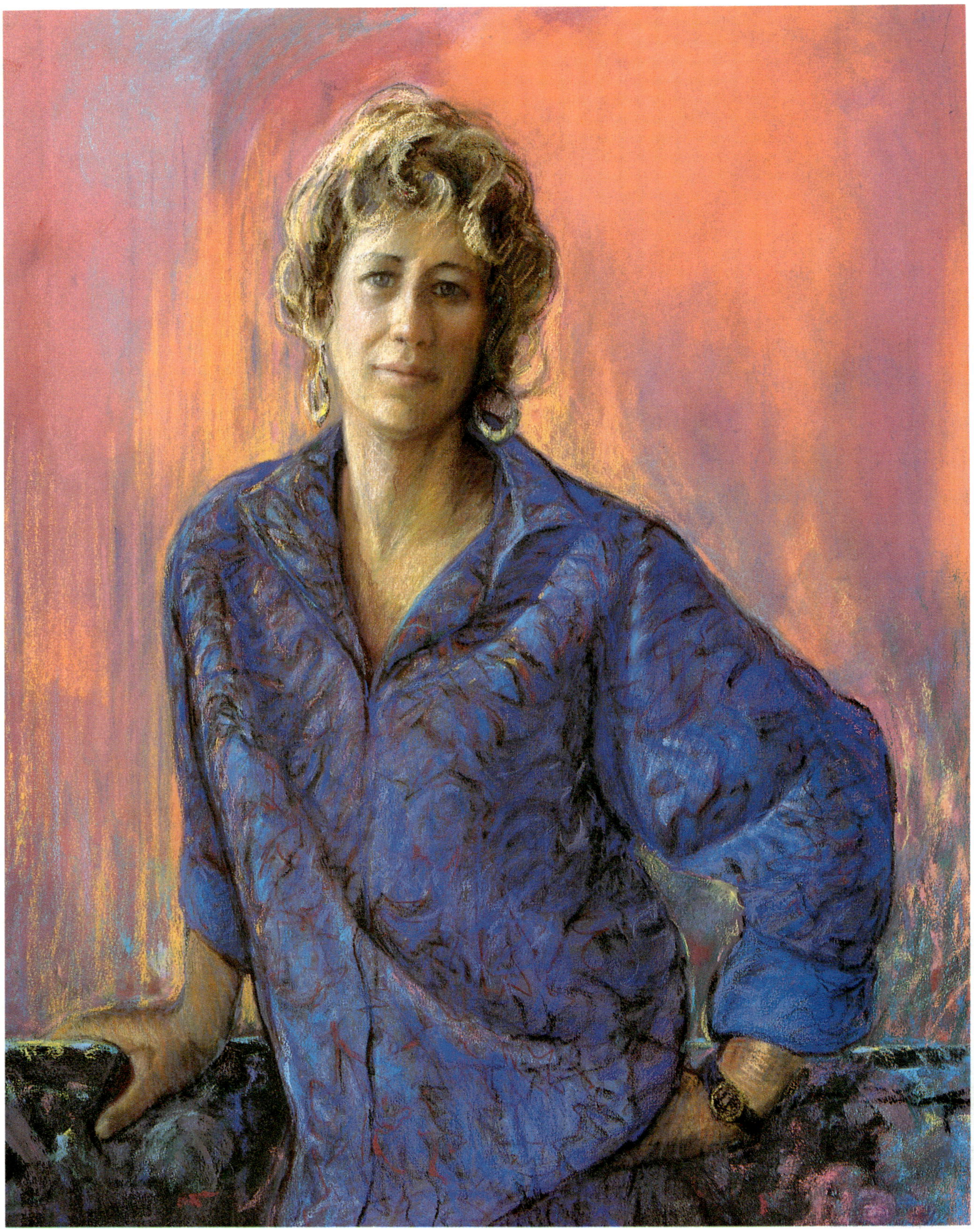

Stephanie Pastel On Canvas 48 x 38

This portrait was painted from life and instant photographs under north light on a canvas toned with a pink pumice/gesso texture. It was intentionally painted slightly larger than life-size for impact.

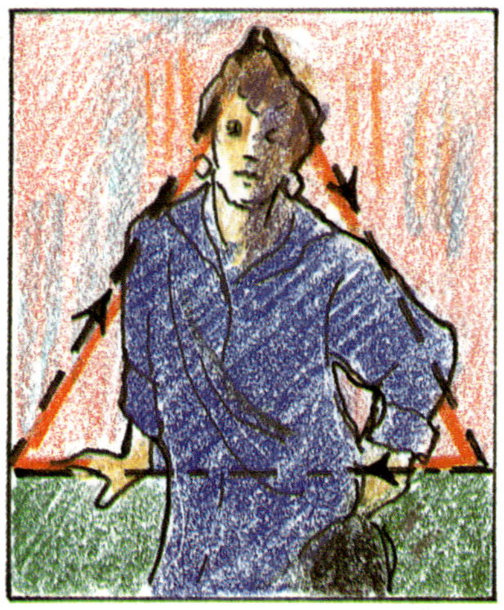

One way to create impact on either large- or small-scale portraits is to use a centralized triangular shape as your center of interest. This diagram shows how the eye follows a triangular path from base to apex and then back to the base. Subconsciously, the viewer gains a sense of strength from this shape because it is one of nature's most stable forms.

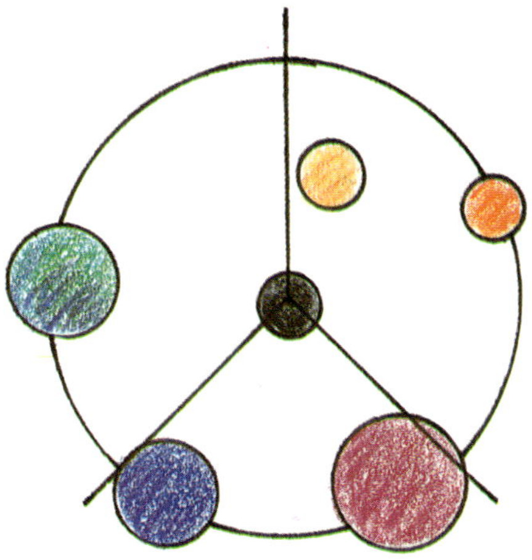

If size and triangular composition alone were not enough to create impact, the color and form simplification of all major areas in this portrait would guarantee it. The background is large, and the green and pink complementary colors make horizontal and vertical contrasts; the blue shirt is a strong, simple shape; the cool, light flesh tones contrast with the warm shadow side; and the hair has a simple light/dark pattern.

CONVEYING A MOOD

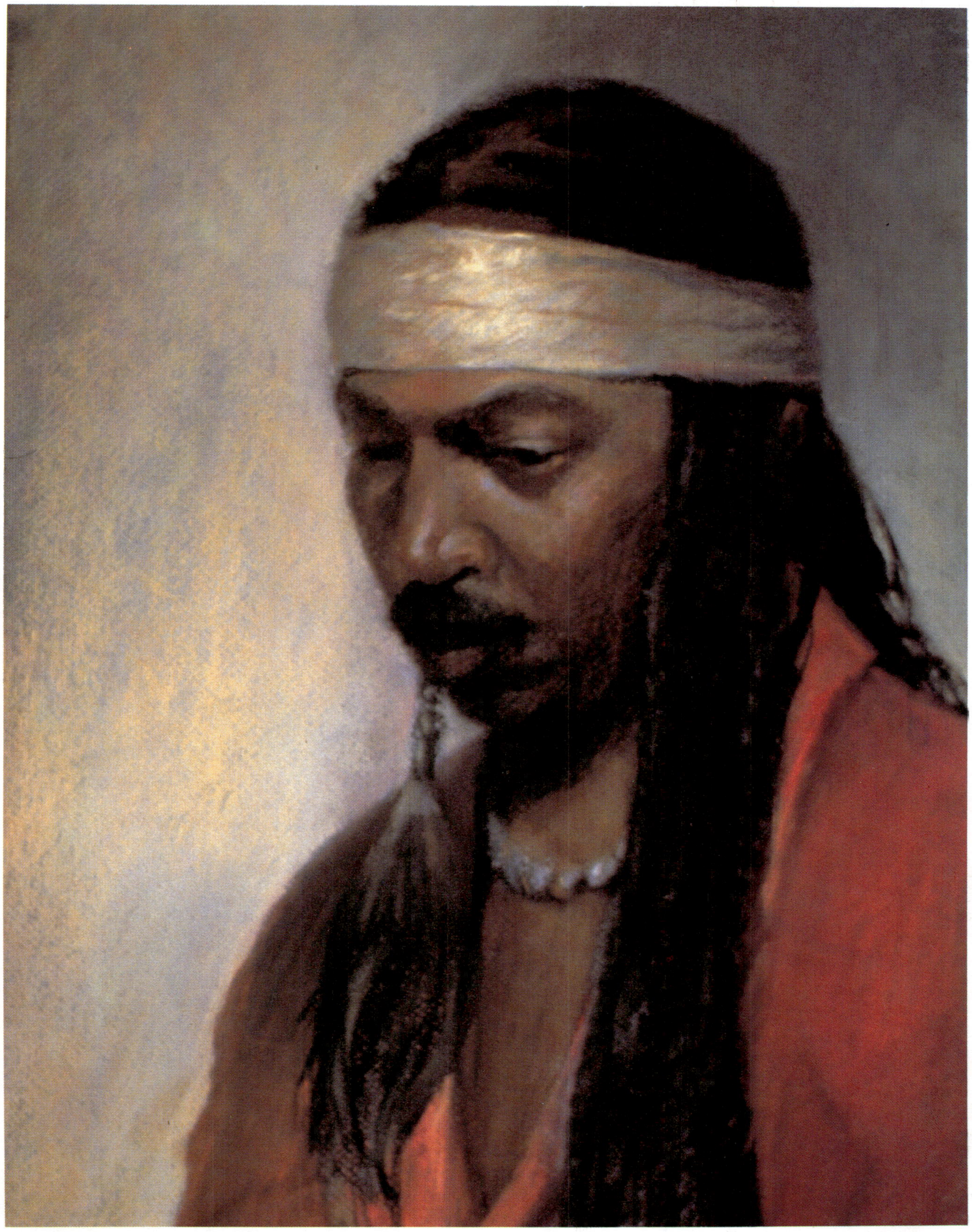

Robert Pastel On Gray Paper 22 x 16

Often the best poses are taken during breaks when your model is relaxed, neither of you has expectations, and, of course, you don't have a camera. However, there are rare times when you are setting the model and you suddenly find a pose that is perfect because it conveys a definite mood. Then the question is, "How do you capture that special feeling along with a likeness?"

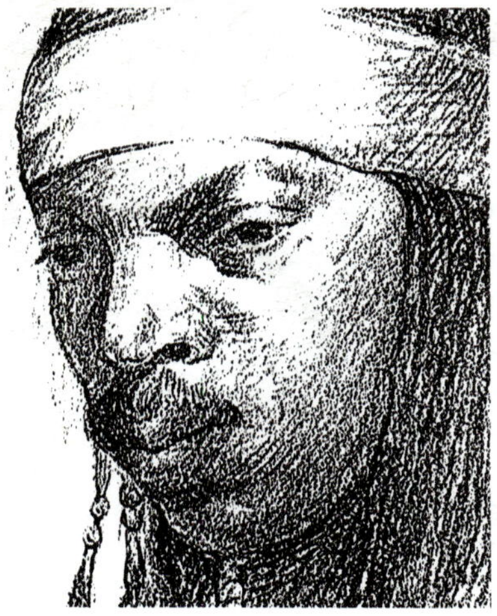

When you sense something special about a pose, do not rush to begin. Instead, look harder than ever at the gesture, colors, and lighting in hopes of pinpointing the essence to which you are attracted. In this case, the somber colors are a part of the appeal, but, more than that, there is something compelling about the gaze. This detail, one of many preliminary drawings, shows how closely you can study a gesture before finally going into color.

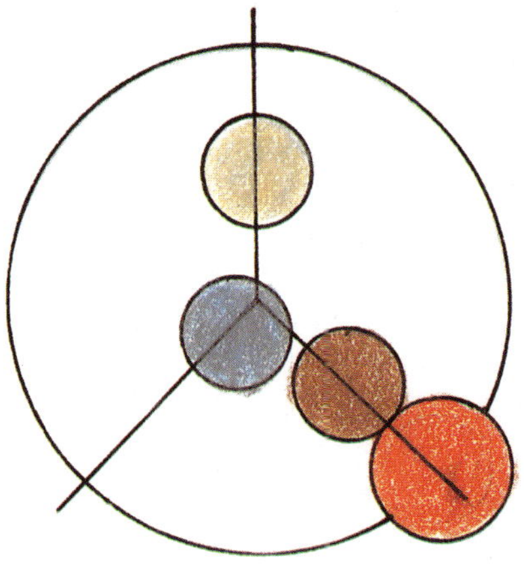

When you are trying to convey a color mood, it is important to look very hard and attempt to record the color relationships just as they appear. In terms of the color wheel, this pose is almost monochromatic with low-key grays and browns that are accented by the red shirt. Since most of the colors are low key, they add a somber quality to Robert's somewhat reflective gaze. This portrait was painted under a diffused north skylight on an overcast day.

SELF-PORTRAITS: YOU ARE YOUR OWN BEST MODEL

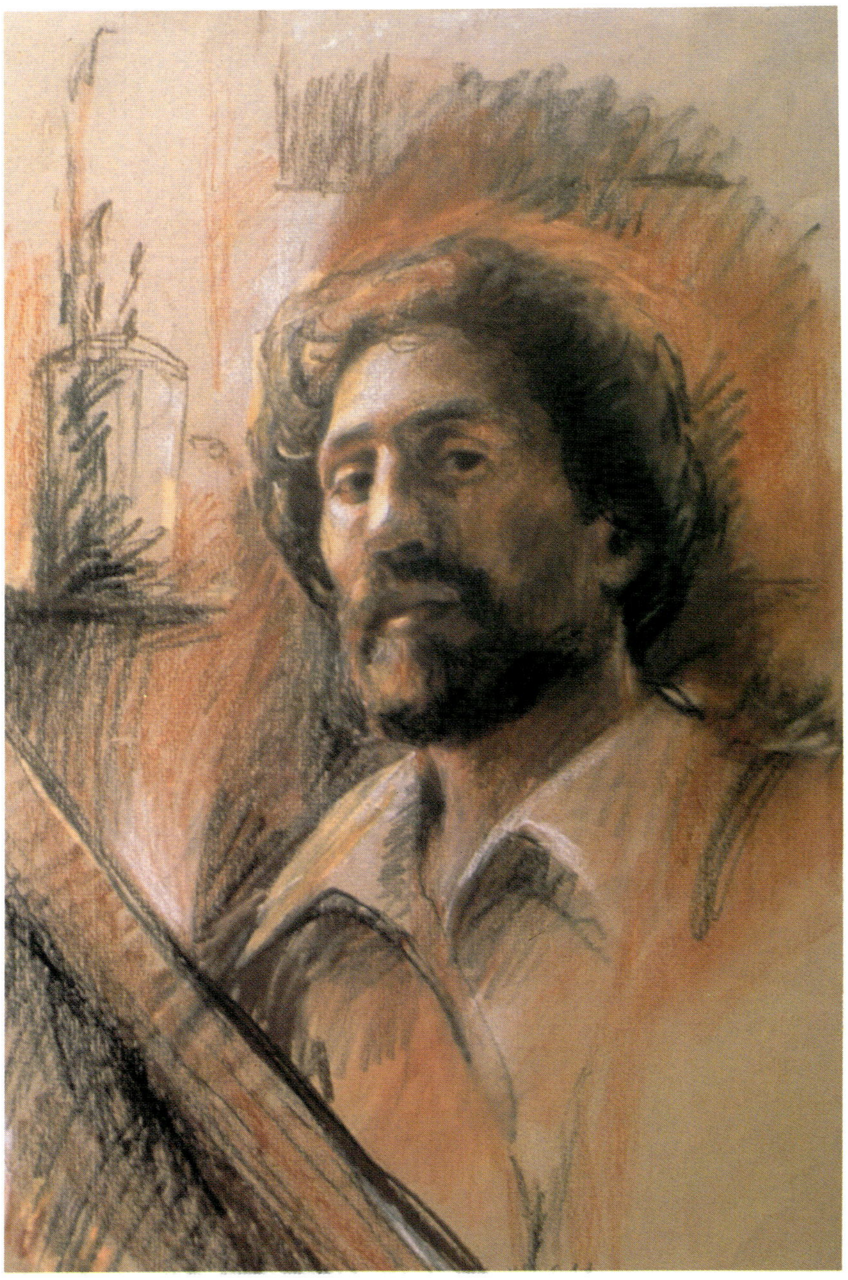

Self-portrait Browns, Black, And White On Gray Paper 16 x 10-1/2

In yourself and your mirror you have a model who is the epitome of cooperation. You are always on time, no hour is too early or late, and there is no limit to the expressions you can hold.

The studio setup shown in the photo below is an example of how to set up your own self-portrait area. This self-portrait was done on a mid-tone grayish paper with the chalks shown below which give a full range of values.

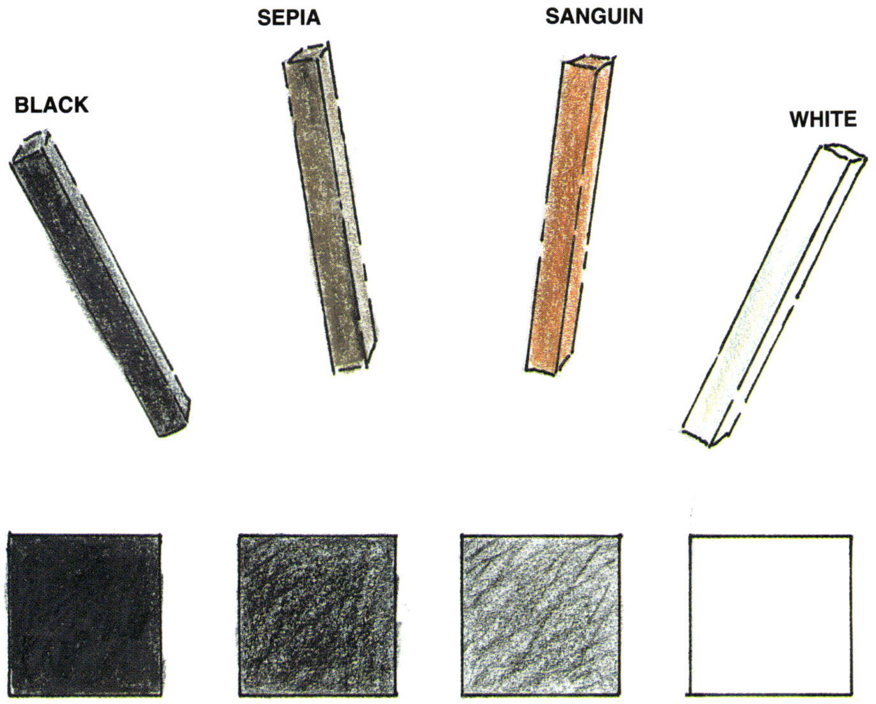

ODD ANGLES AND SIMPLE MATERIALS

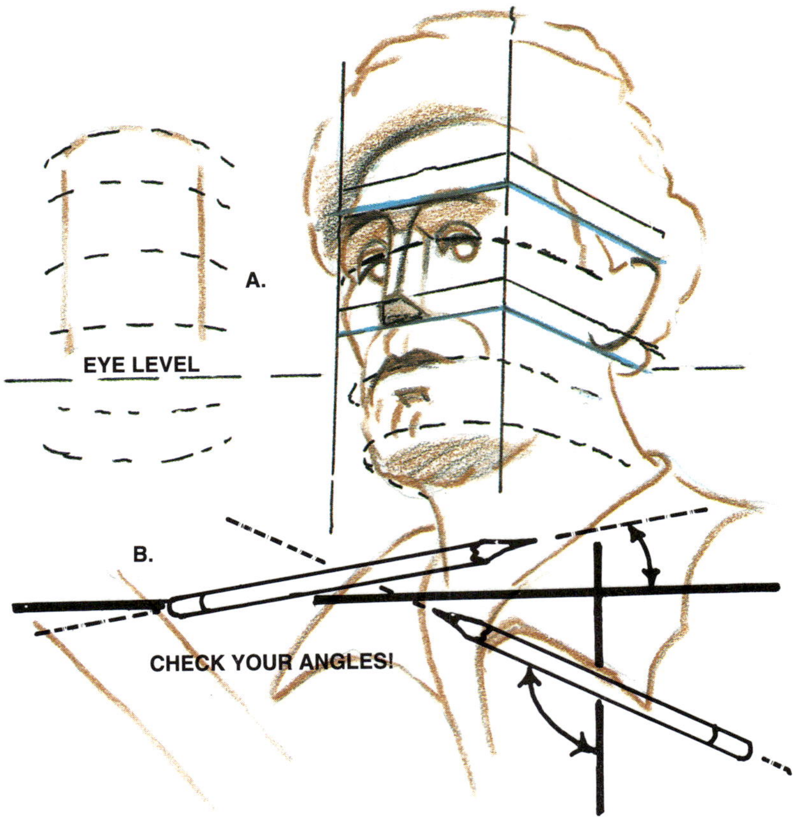

Self-portraits give you the luxury of experimenting with many strange angles and expressions that a sitter might not care to hold. Try drawing your head in various positions; use a second or third mirror for profiles. Practice with natural light during the day and spot or fluorescent lights at night. The diagram above shows how to use correct perspective when your head is tilted back and your features are seen from below. Notice that a head follows the same laws of perspective as a cube or cylinder (A). The secret of perspective is to correctly draw each angle of the forms you see in proper relation to a horizontal and vertical axis (B). Use your pencil to check these angles.

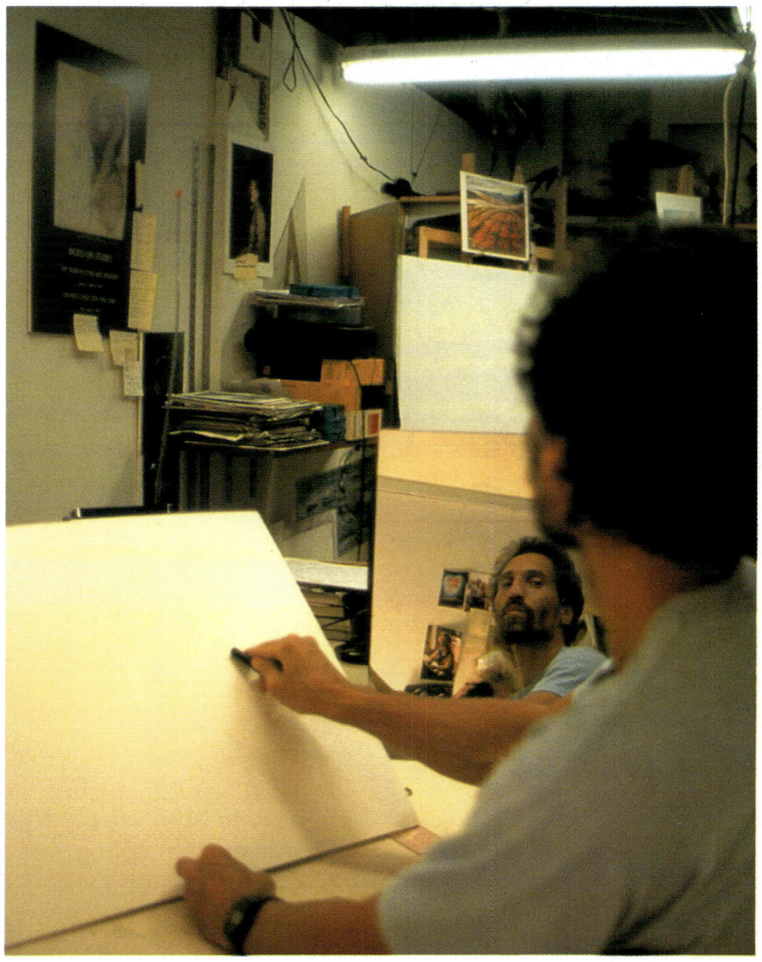

A setup for self-portraits under fluorescent light.

SELF-PORTRAITS: LIFE-SIZE AND FULL-COLOR

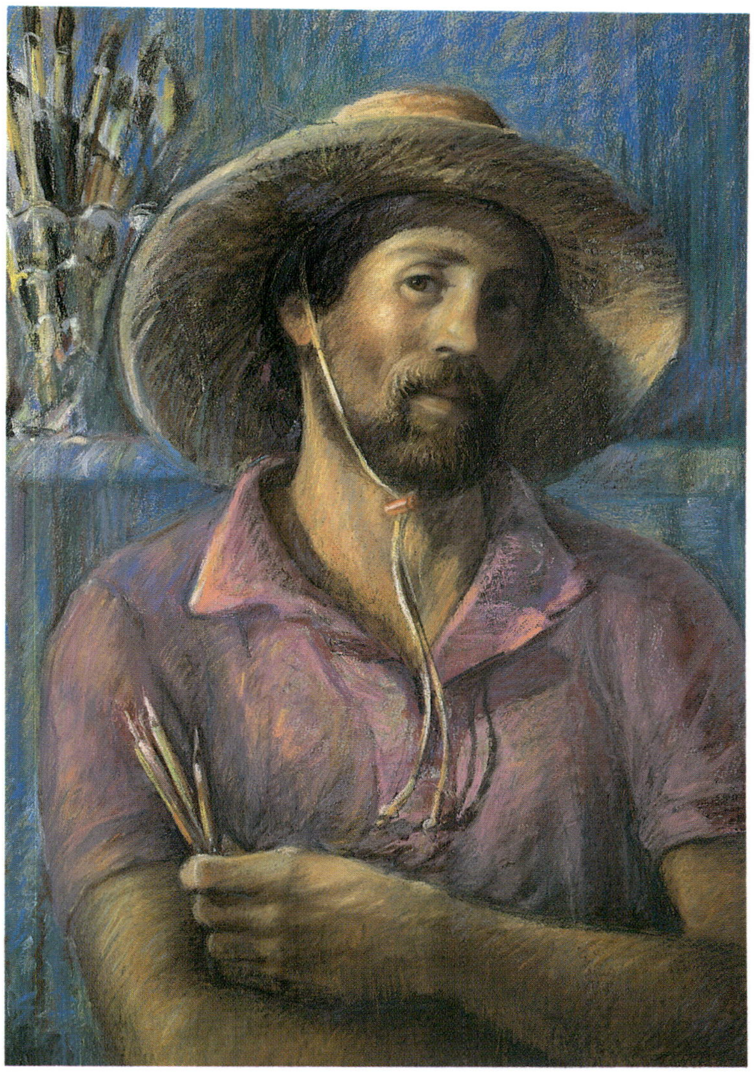

Self-portrait *Pastel On Pumice/Gesso Canvas* *44 x 36*

When you do a self-portrait that shows the hand you normally work with, it forces you to look hard, analyze what you see, and use your memory to record the information. By the look of this self-portrait, you would think I was left-handed, but I'm not. Remember, the mirror reverses everything. We seldom see ourselves as others see us.

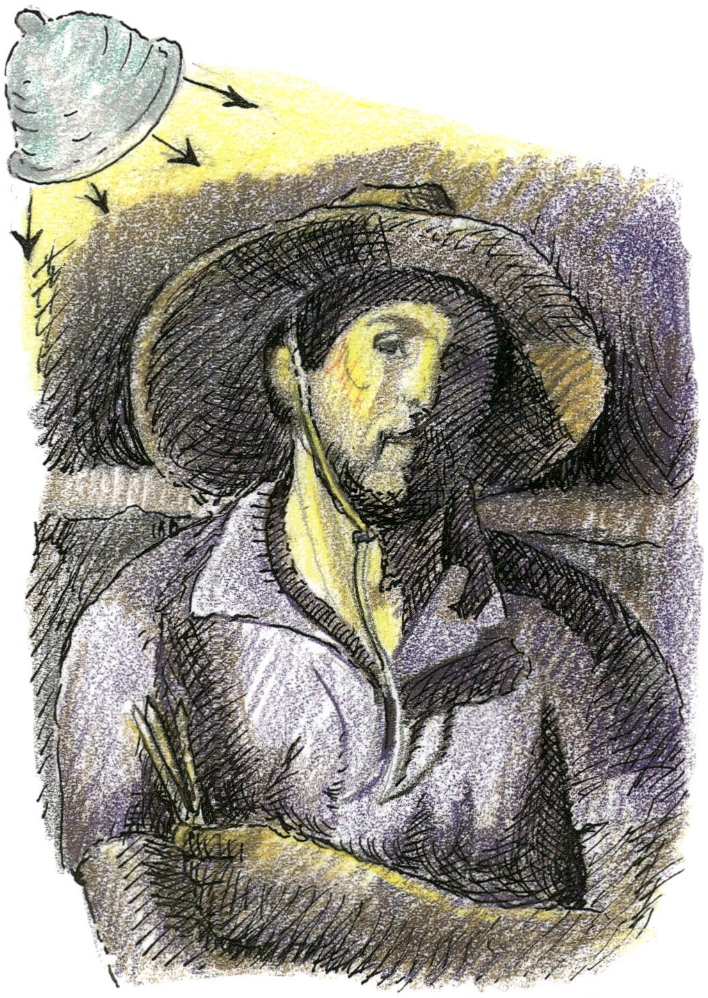

The light in this self-portrait comes from a traditional angle (45° high and off to the side), which is good for showing volume. My landscape painting hat throws an interesting cast shadow, and its yellowish tone works well in relation to the red-violet shirt and blue background (these are split-complements to yellow). To paint in full color, you must first see values. Squint your eyes at the two-colored drawing above (this is like looking through a piece of smoked Plexiglas). Notice how there are three main values—the background and shadows are a dark value; the shirt is a middle value; and the light face (accented with darks) becomes a center of interest.

The mirror is hinged to a wall so its angle can be changed. This mirror is an old one, but it does the job.

In this photo you can see other portraits as well as a landscape study. You might want to work on more than one project at a time to keep your eyes fresh.

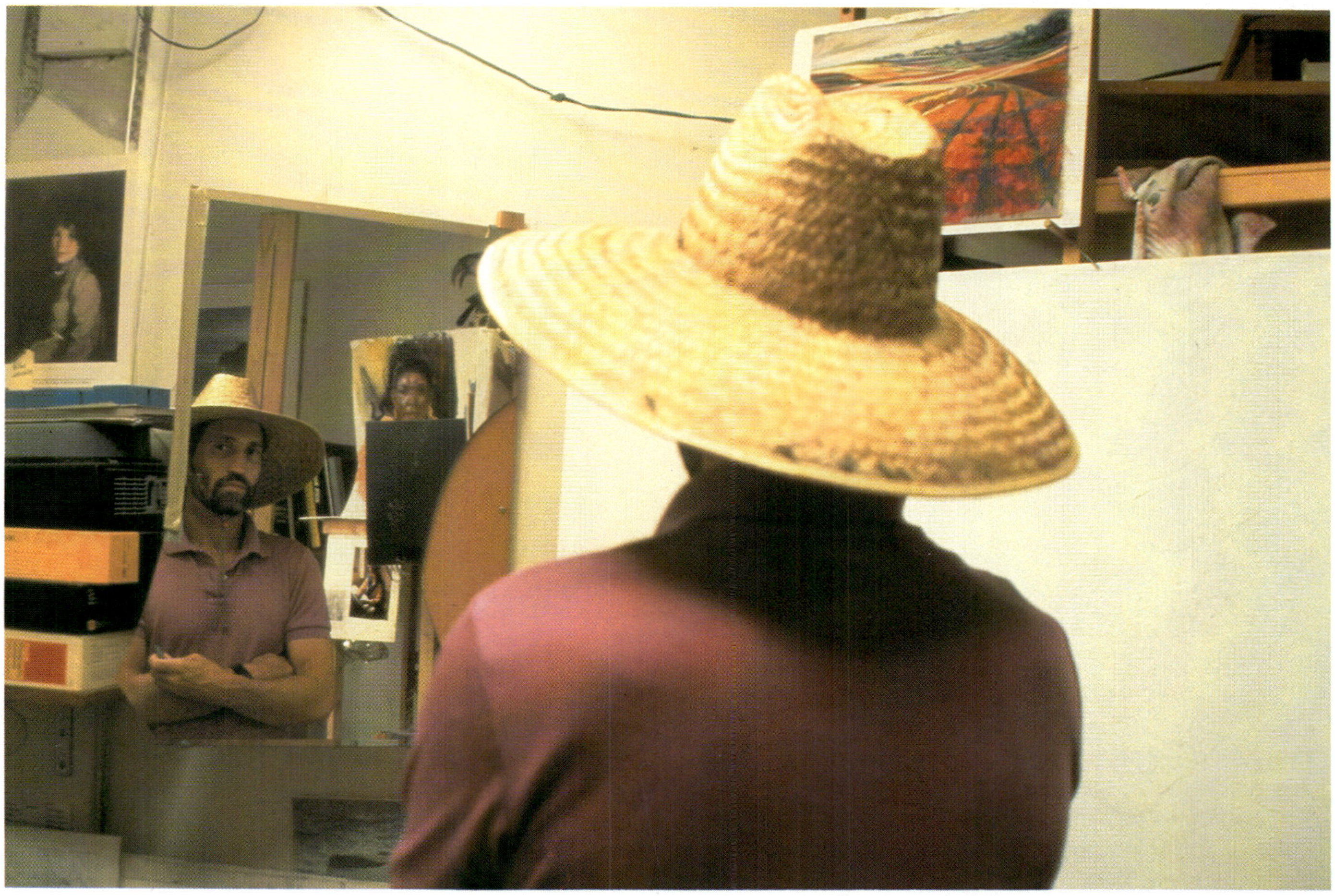

This is a typical setup for doing life-size self-portraits.

LEARN BY COPYING THE MASTERS

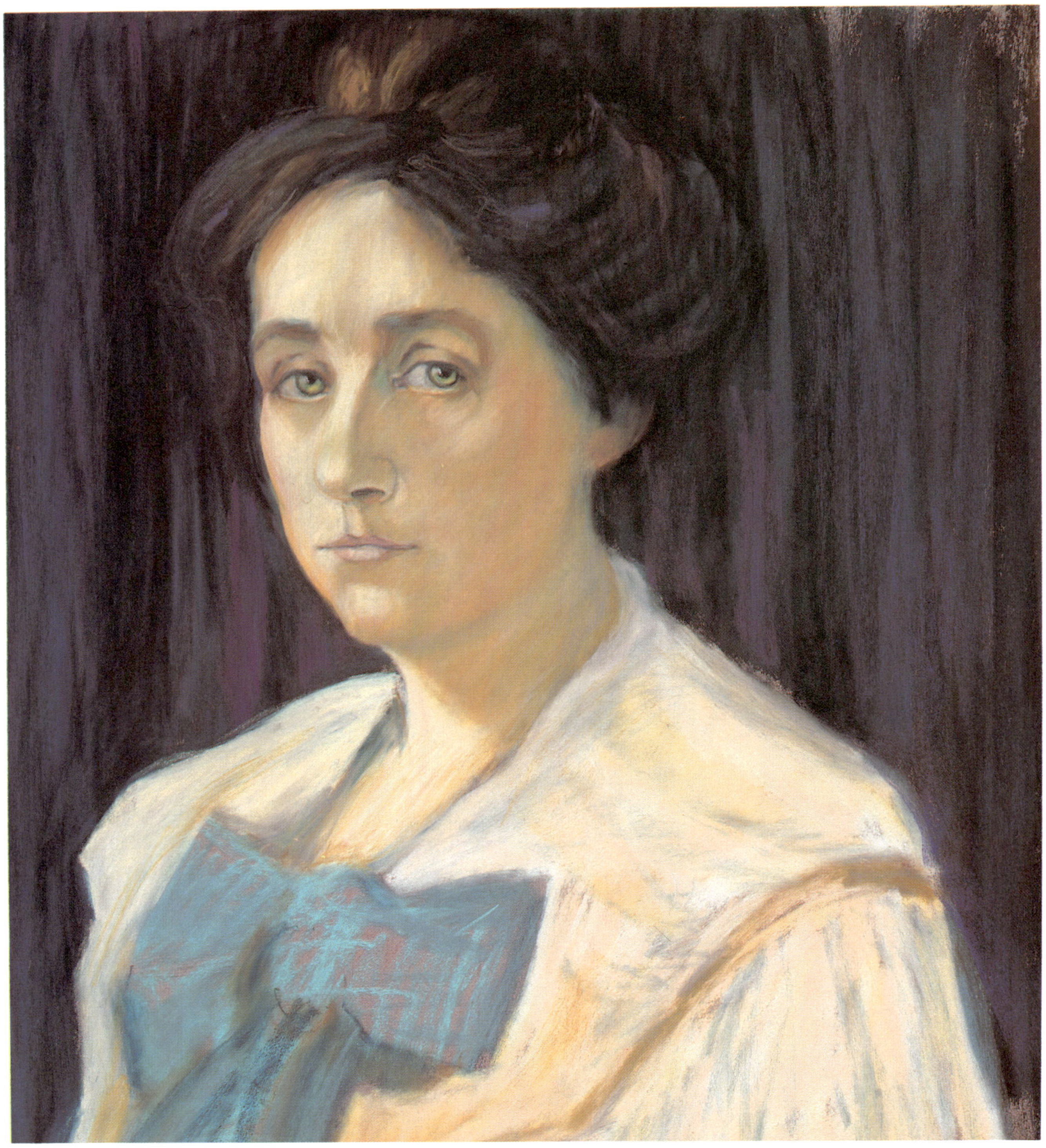

Gabriella Munter (After Wassily Kandinsky Oil) Copied In Pastel On Blue Pumice Board 19 x 18

Most people know Kandinsky for his abstract art, but he was also well-versed in portraiture and landscape painting. Like most artists, he copied other masters to gain greater skill and understanding.

Using some of the insights given below, try making your own version of this portrait. Remember, understanding the underlying principles of this work is more important than simply achieving a likeness.

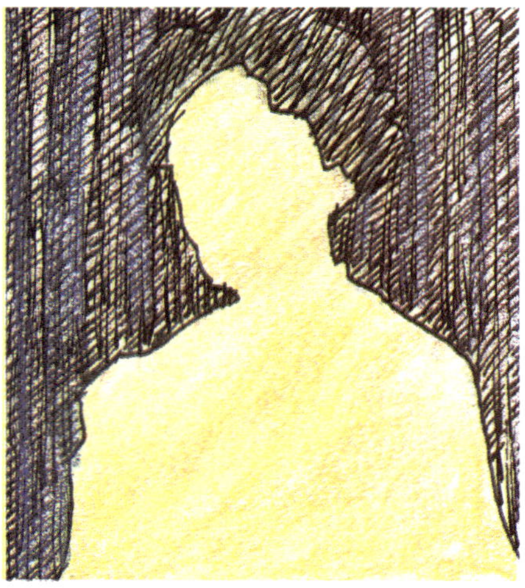

Placement—The negative space around this portrait is interesting in its own right. Notice how each of the four corners is slightly different than the others. The background's vertical emphasis adds interest to this nearly square format.

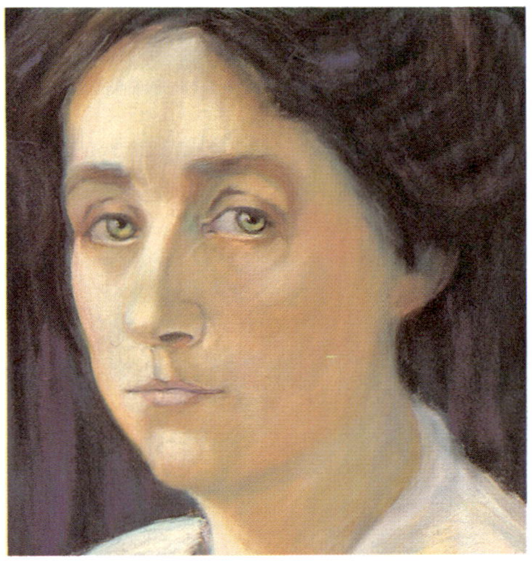

Color—The lighting here is a cool diffused natural light so the shadow is soft and warm. There are many greens, pinks, and raw siennas in both the shadow and light flesh tones, but extra raw sienna in the shadow side keeps it the warmest.

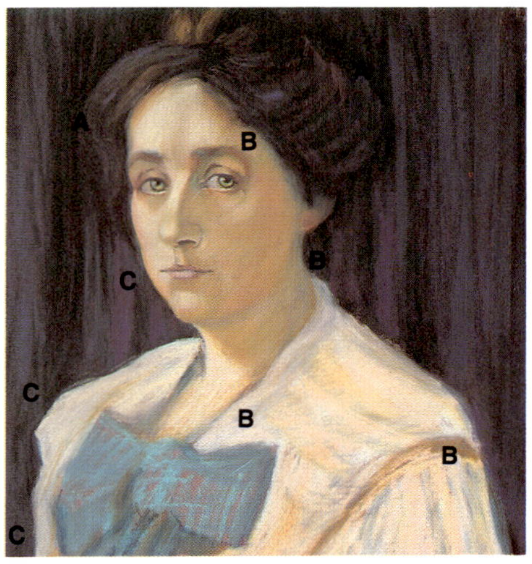

Observations—Look for (A) lost edges, (B) medium edges, and (C) hard edges (light-facing side). Notice the careful rendering of the sphere-shaped eyes (center of interest) and the three-tone value system—**light**: blouse, face; **mid-tone**: bow, eyes; **dark**: hair, background.

DO A SELF-PORTRAIT; STUDY A MASTER; CREATE A COMPOSITION

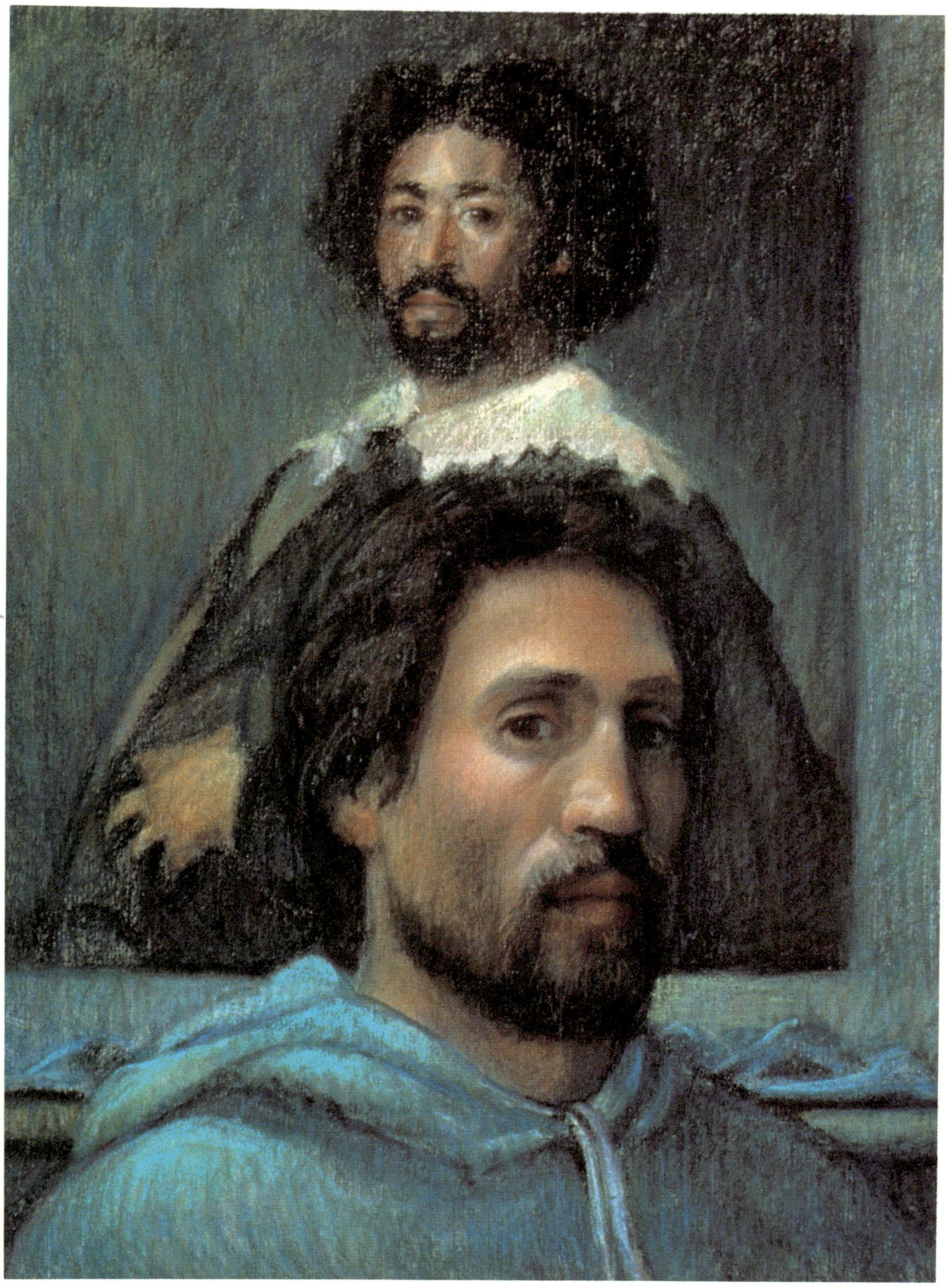

"Homage To Velazquez" *Portrait Of Juan de Pareja Pastel On Gray Canvas 24 x 18*

When you copy the masters' works—searching for the *reasons* they did certain things—and then compare them to your own work, you are bridging time and allowing their methods to rub off on you. The intensity of studying in this way and combining it with a self-portrait that has a similar mood is an excellent way to break old habits, gain new insights, and create an interesting picture.

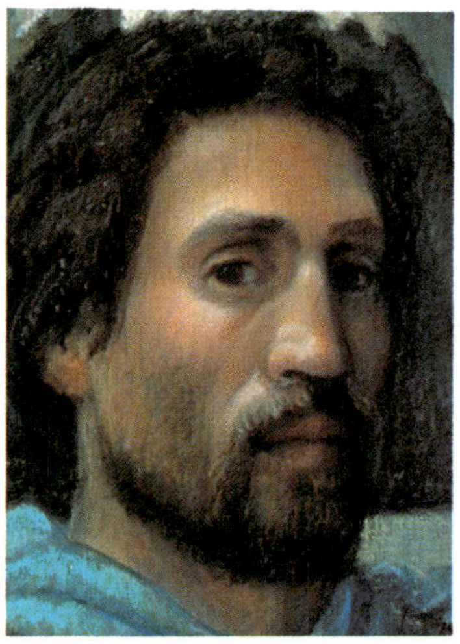

In keeping with the mood of Velazquez's portrait, which is based on a very limited palette, the flesh colors are deliberately toned down with cool greens and grays. Black is used for some darks, but another color is always applied over it to give it life.

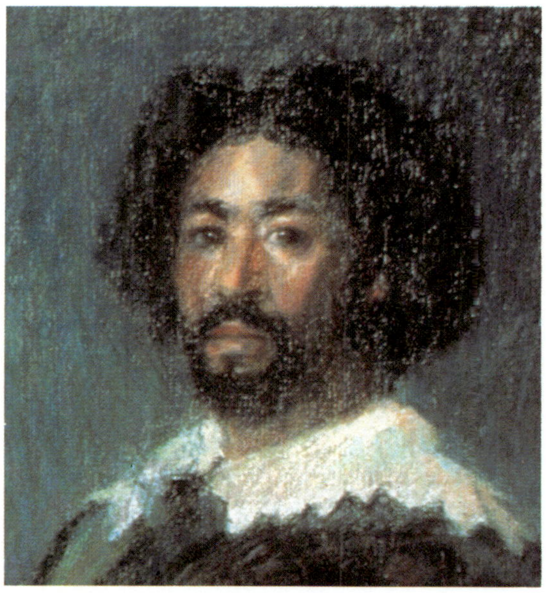

The lighting on Juan's face is almost frontal; it is based on the way light and shadow reveal volume on spheres and rectangles.

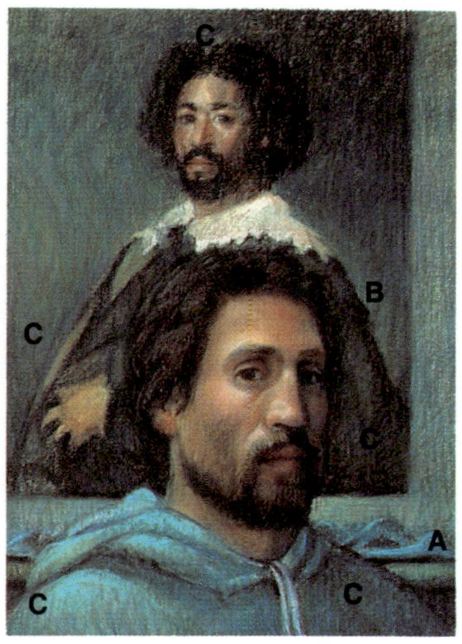

The colors here are red and blue-green toned down with a scumbled gray glaze. Compositionally, the horizontals (A) and verticals (B) stabilize the picture by adding a contrast of straight to curve (C). Notice the repetition of both portraits' triangular compositions.

PASTEL OVER WATERCOLOR

Watercolor and pastel make a great combination because they are both vibrant, albeit in different ways. Watercolor has the translucent beauty of an atmospheric display, while pastel has an opaque crystalline quality. Each medium can stand alone, but when they are combined they add new dimensions to one another.

For covering large areas, pastels can be time-consuming, dusty, and expensive. On the other hand, watercolors can be easily used to underpaint these areas, laying an immediate foundation for dark darks, crisp edges, and bright lights. The three paintings shown on the right are finished watercolors that do not require pastel. For underpainting, you need not do a finished watercolor; just block in big areas of color and try to get your values right. Page 2 lists the necessary supplies for watercolors; page 4 explains how to stretch the watercolor paper.

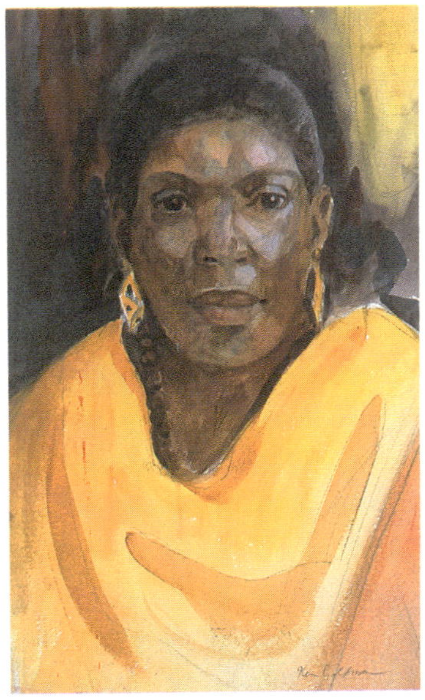

Strong darks and lights create drama. No white paint was used. Notice the blue-gray highlights.

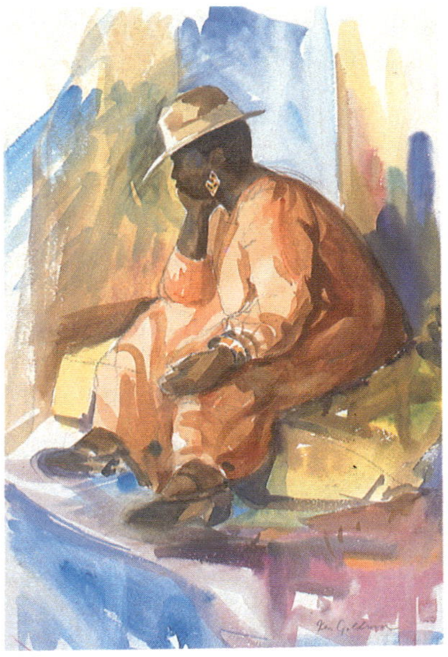

The silhouetted dark head and sparkling earring make for a definite center of interest.

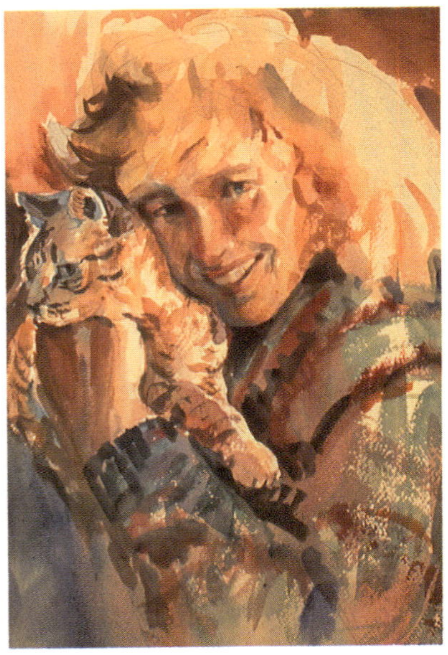

Part of the arm is dry-brushed and some of it is wet-into-wet. Experiment. You can always add pastel.

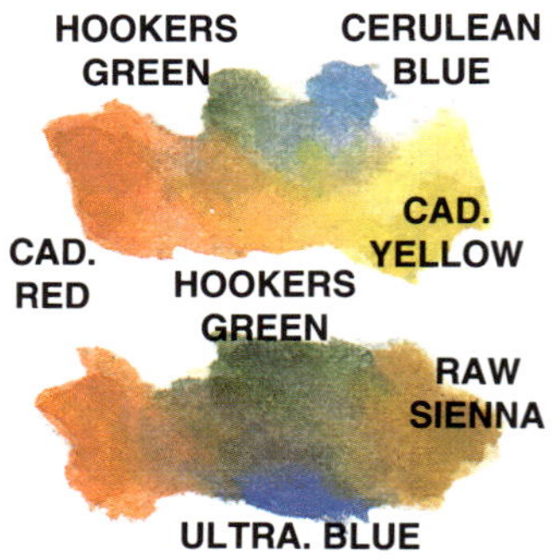

These colors can work for flesh tones of any racial group. The main difference is in the proportions; i.e., the shadows on fair skin should be the same mixture as the lightest area of darker skin.

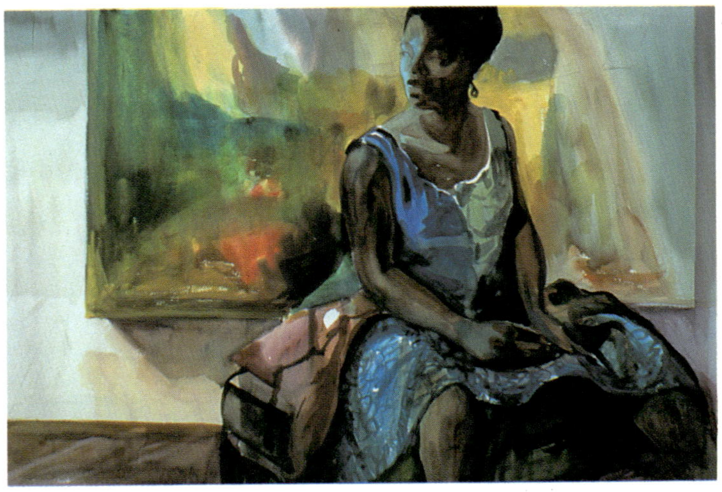

An overworked watercolor painting makes a good underpainting for pastels.

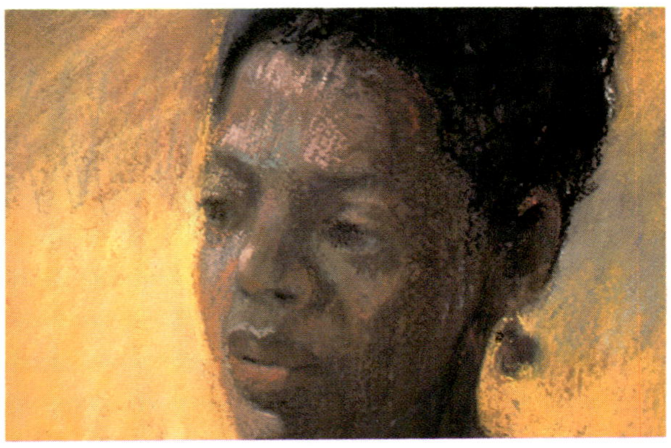

On this detail you can see how pastel stays on the "hills" of paper texture, while the watercolor underpainting stays in the "valleys." The colorful strokes of pastel re-enlivened the watercolor.

The watercolor painting above is overworked and in need of clarification. Redrawing the basic shapes, changing the composition, and enhancing the colors with pastels shows how well opaque chalk can both correct and complement a watercolor. This portrait (right) was done on stretched 140 lb. cold-press (semi-rough) paper. You can get a heavier weight paper, such as 300 lb., so that stretching is unnecessary, but it is more expensive.

The stages for developing this painting are similar to those on the next page, except that the watercolor flesh tones used for this portrait appear more naturalistic.

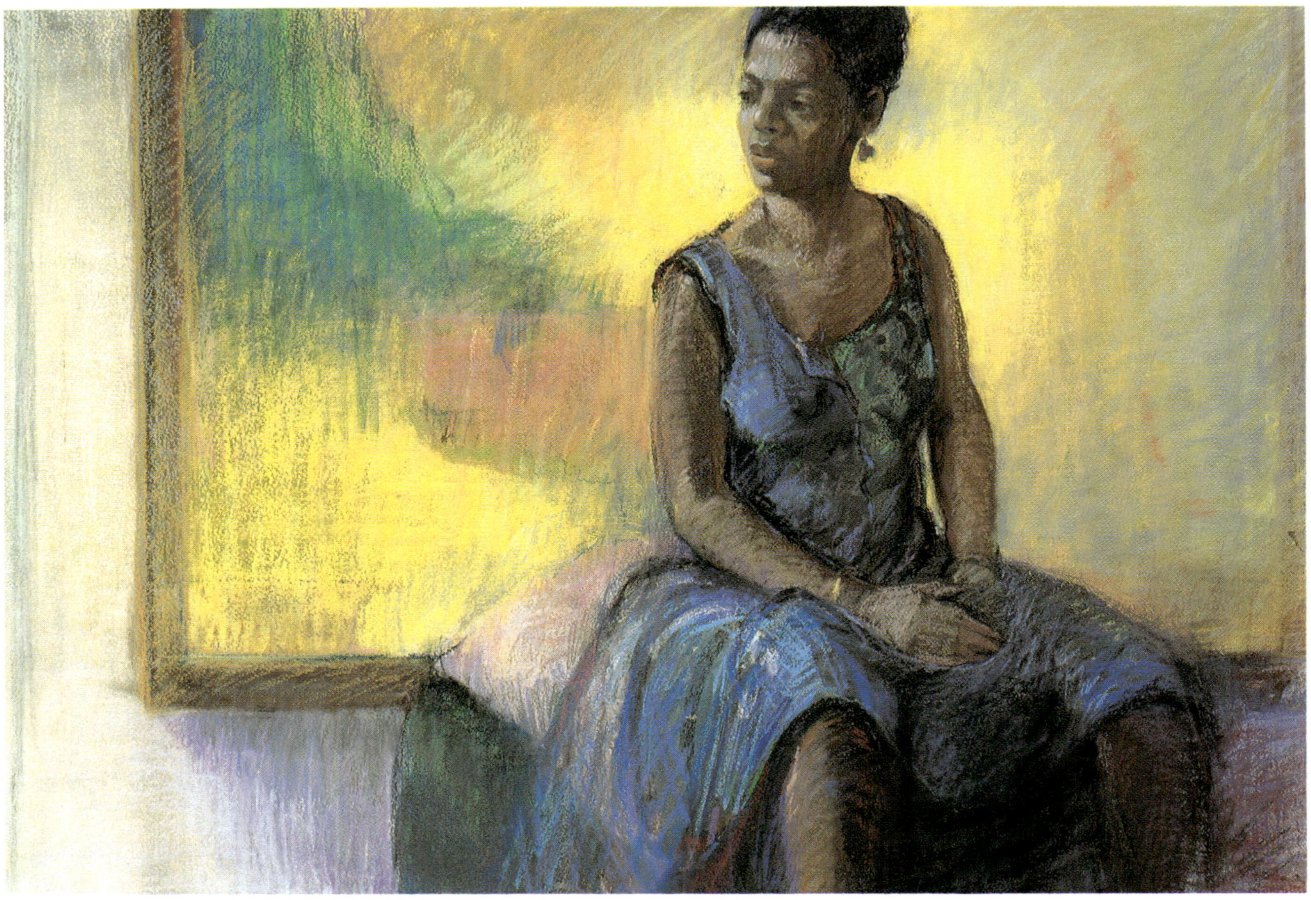

Dorothy Pastel And Watercolor On Paper 24 x 36

PASTEL OVER WATERCOLOR: PROCESS

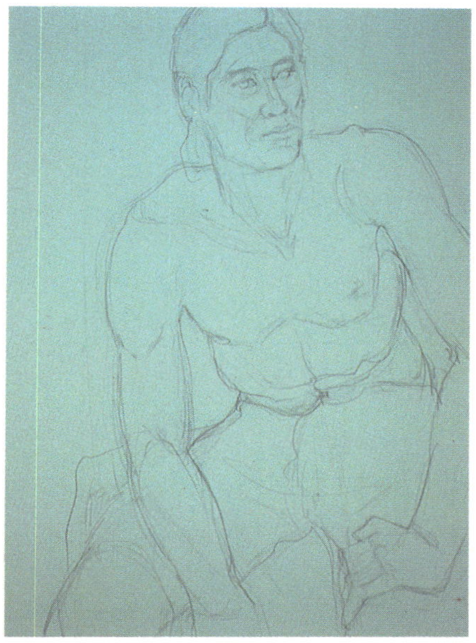

Use a soft graphite pencil and a kneaded eraser to sketch the figure. Pay attention to placement and negative shapes.

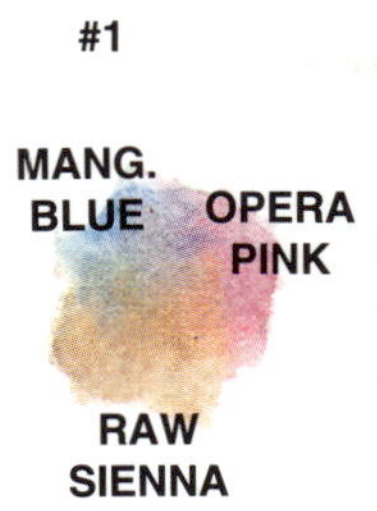

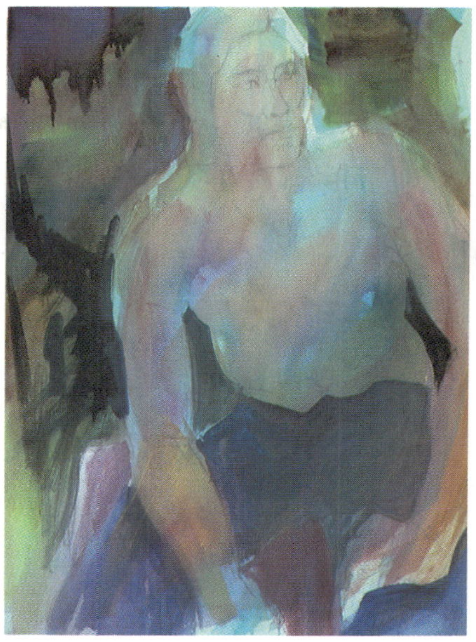

Block in the local colors (wet-into-wet)—#1 for flesh and #2 for darks. First put down blue, then pink, and then raw sienna.

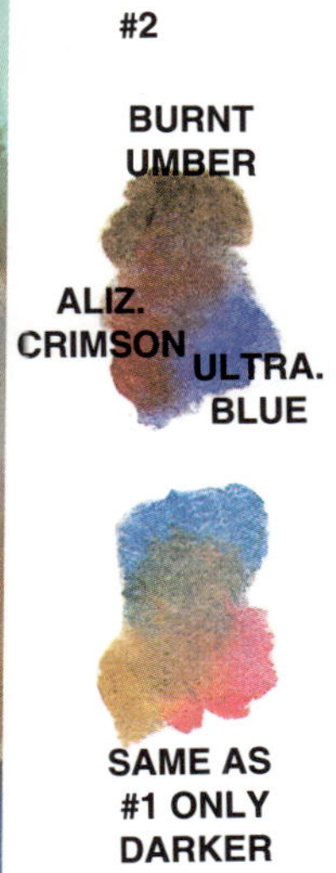

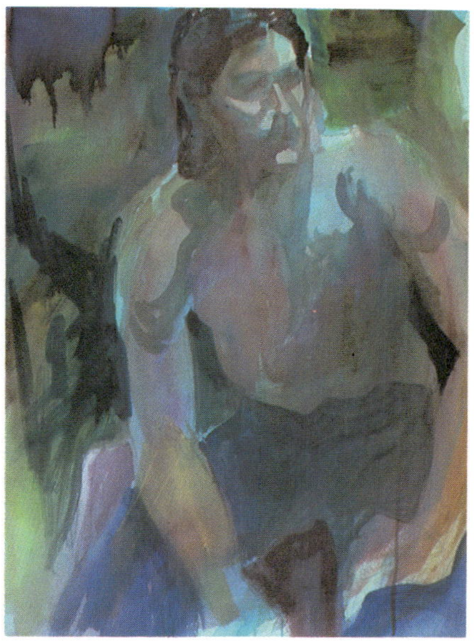

Using colors #2 and #3, mass in shadows and darken the hair and background.

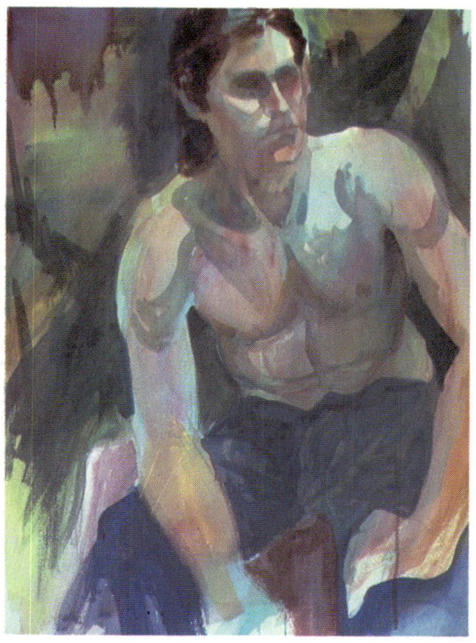

Darken the shadows, hair, and background again. Remember, this is not meant to be a finished watercolor, just an underpainting.

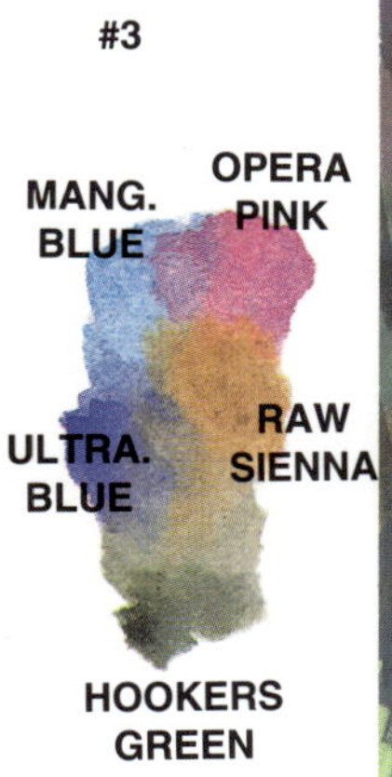

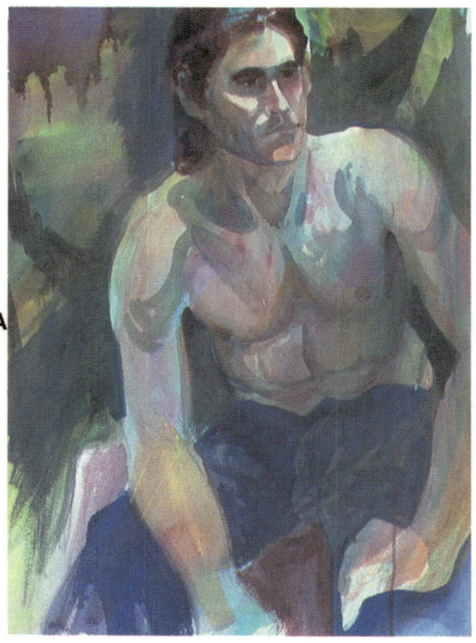

Add dark accents, such as the nostrils, pupils, and lip line. Strengthen the side planes of the face and jaw.

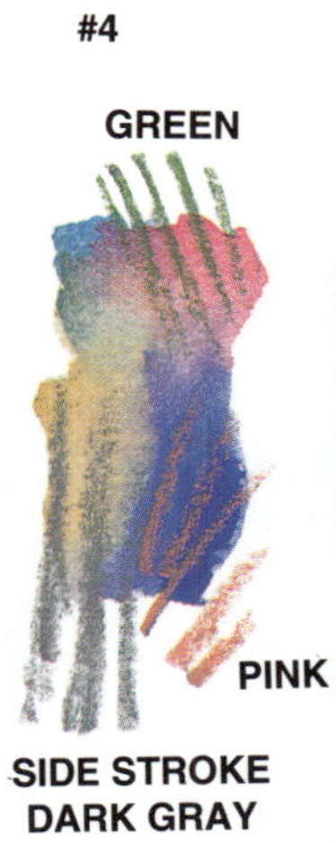

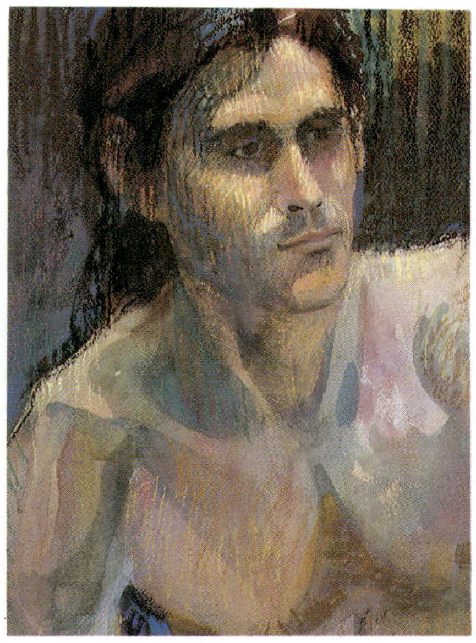

Warm pastel strokes enliven cool areas and vice versa, but don't use too many or the sparkle of contrast will be lost.

This portrait was done under a spotlight, so the light is warm and the shadows are cool. The easel is tilted up at about 60° so the watercolor can run down freely. If you decide to try a portrait like this, remember the following pointers: (1) When you mix the colors that are shown above, the colors are mixed wet-into-wet on the paper—not on the palette. (2) Whichever color is put down last will be the dominant tone of the mixture; i.e., when manganese blue is laid down first, then pink, then raw sienna, the mixture will have a dominant raw sienna quality, even though other colors were used. (3) Between each stage, allow the painting to dry completely, and then reapply the next layer of color a little darker. (4) When you add pastels at the end, use them mostly to brighten up dull areas, to lighten overly dark areas, or as linear accents (see page 5) to add character and volume. Since the background was personalized to harmonize with *this* figure, you might want to make up your own as well.

Peter Watercolor On Paper 30 x 22

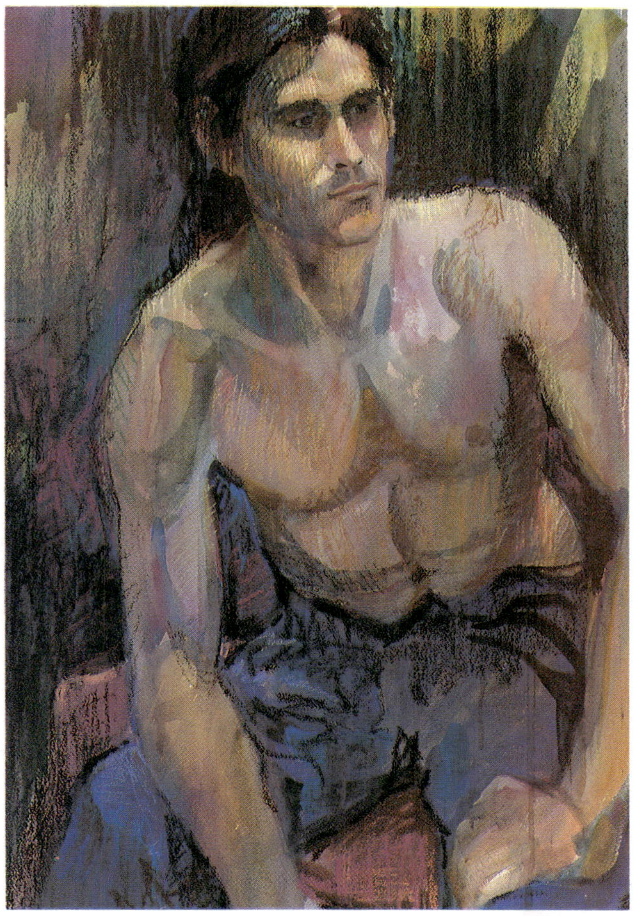

WATERCOLOR AND BLACK PASTEL PENCIL: LESS IS MORE

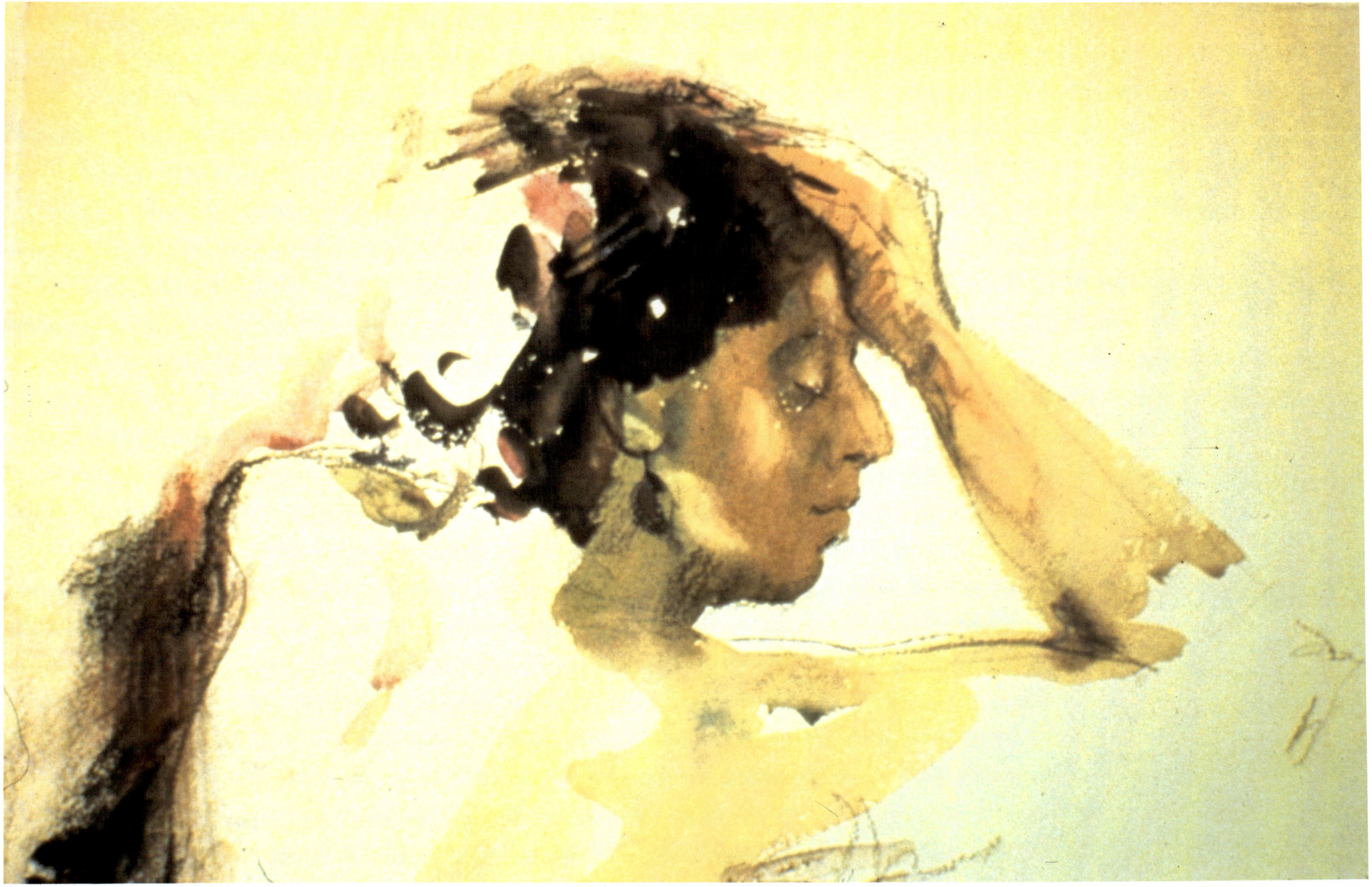

Before you set a model for an extended session, it can be helpful to do several quick poses for warm-ups. One, five, fifteen, and twenty minutes are all good practice for quickly seeing relationships and trying to capture only the essentials. This profile study was sketched in with a pastel pencil on a half-sheet of unstretched rough watercolor paper during a 20-minute pose (set on a timer). Within five minutes, the essential lines were completed and the watercolor stage was begun. The shadow areas were given color, while the light flesh was left as white paper. Three colors—cadmium red, raw sienna, and cerulean blue—were used for the shadow flesh (see page 28); burnt sienna and ultramarine blue were used for the dark hair; magenta was used for accents. After the washes had almost dried, black pastel pencil was reintroduced to accent eyes, nostrils, hand, and back...then the timer went off. This kind of exercise will help you loosen up and strengthen your eye/hand coordination.

USING INTERIOR SPACE AS DESIGN • CREATING A FOCAL POINT

CONNECTIONS

Constantly look from subject to background to subject again. This will help you to see relative proportions and overall connections. In this diagram, horizontal direction (A) lines up with (B), stabilizing the picture's base; it is then echoed in (C). Verticals (D, E, F, G) reinforce the gesture, while diagonal (H) brings attention back into the picture.

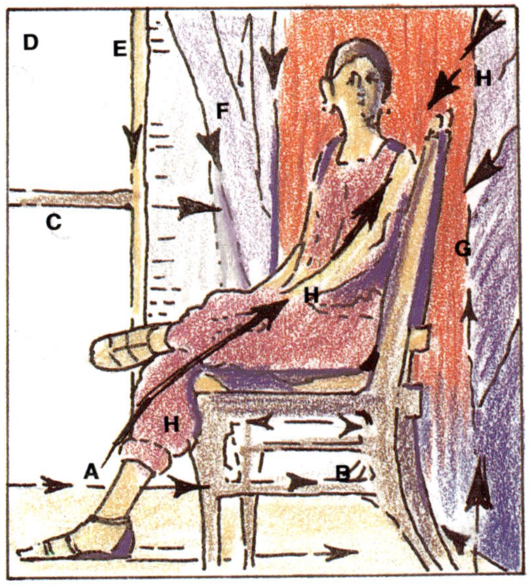

FOCAL POINT

Here are some elements that help make Christina the center of interest:

Hue—More variety of color on and around the figure.

Chroma—The most intense colors are on and around the figure.

Value—Lightest lights meet darkest darks on the figure.

Temperature—Warm/cool contrasts are most extreme on the figure.

Shape—The rounded, soft forms of the figure contrast the straight rectangular forms in the background.

Direction—Diagonals, verticals, and horizontals converge on the figure.

Texture—The patterns on the clothing are quite different from the textures behind the figure.

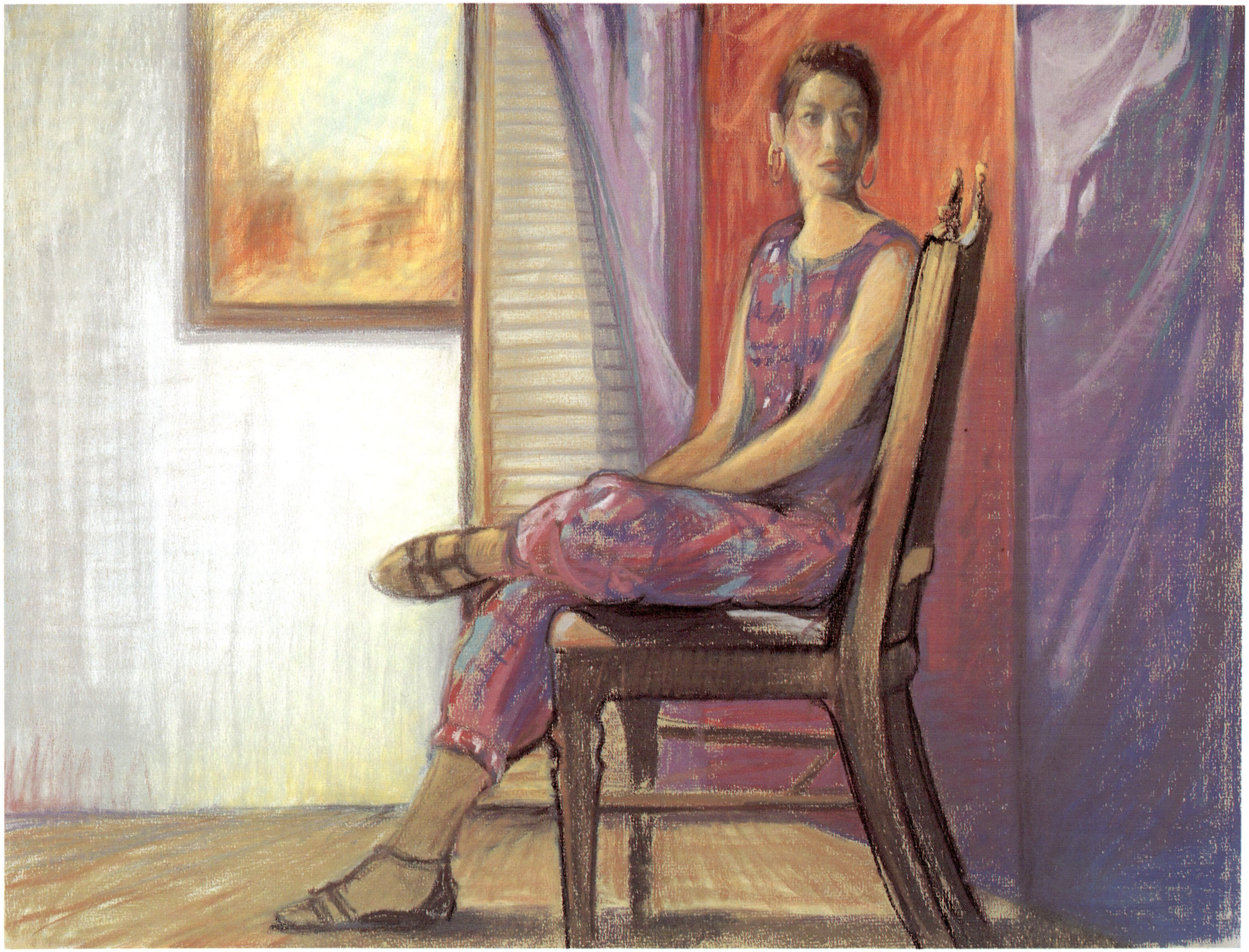

Christina Pastel On Tan Paper 18 x 24

When you first set your model, the background should be arranged in such a way that it adds dynamic tension to the pose. While you're developing the portrait and trying to find correct proportions, it is important to lightly draw all the connections between foreground and background as you really see them. Toward the end, if it seems necessary, you can rearrange some horizontals, verticals, or diagonals to strengthen the composition. Horizontals (A) and (B) were changed to line up with one another, and the diagonal shadow (H) was lined up with the arm and leg.

Walter Foster Art Instruction Program

THREE EASY STEPS TO LEARNING ART

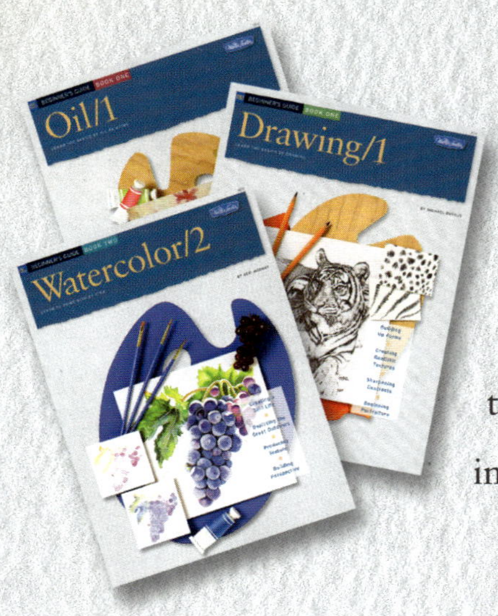

Beginner's Guides are specially written to encourage and motivate aspiring artists. This series introduces the various painting and drawing media—acrylic, oil, pastel, pencil, and watercolor—making it the perfect starting point for beginners. Book One introduces the medium, showing some of its diverse possibilities through beautiful rendered examples and simple explanations, and Book Two instructs with a set of engaging art lessons that follow an easy step-by-step approach.

How to Draw and Paint titles contain progressive visual demonstrations, expert advice, and simple written explanations that assist novice artists through the next stages of learning. In this series, professional artists tap into their experience to walk the reader through the artistic process step by step, from preparation work and preliminary sketches to special techniques and final details. Organized by medium, these books provide insight into an array of subjects.

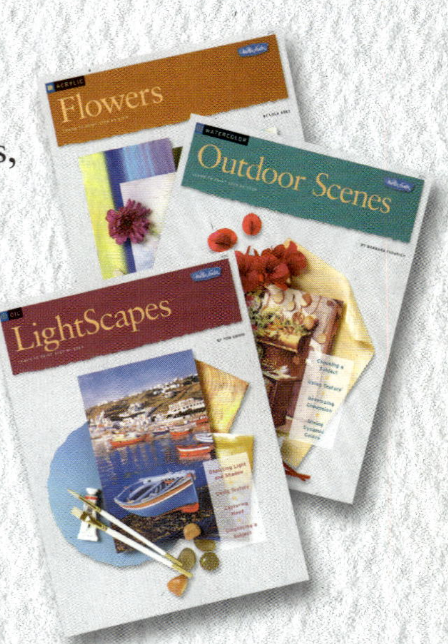

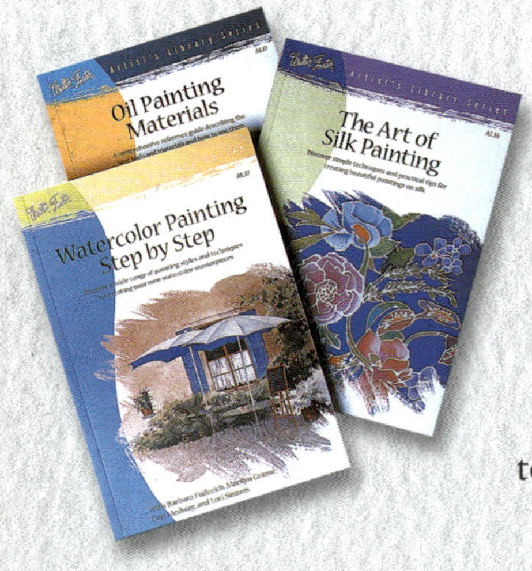

Artist's Library titles offer both beginning and advanced artists the opportunity to expand their creativity, conquer technical obstacles, and explore new media. Written and illustrated by professional artists, the books in this series are ideal for anyone aspiring to reach a new level of expertise. They'll serve as useful tools that artists of all skill levels can refer to again and again.

Walter Foster products are available at art and craft stores everywhere. Write or call for a FREE catalog that includes all of Walter Foster's titles, or visit our website at www.walterfoster.com.

WALTER FOSTER PUBLISHING, INC.
23062 La Cadena Drive
Laguna Hills, California 92653
Main Line 949/380-7510
Toll Free 800/426-0099

www.walterfoster.com